Christ in the Indian Villages

Christ in the Indian Villages

THE RIGHT REV. V. S. AZARIAH, LL.D.

and

THE RT. REV. HENRY WHITEHEAD, D.D.

GYAN

Published by

GYAN

Gyan Publishing House
5, Ansari Road
Daryaganj, New Delhi-110002
Phone: 011-47034999, 9811692060
E-mail: books@gyanbooks.com

Distribution Network
gyanbooks.com
India, USA, Canada, UK, Australia, France

ISBN: 978-81-212-9420-1 (PB)
First Published, 1930

2nd Impression 2023

Printed at: Gyan Press, Delhi.

Christ in the IndianVillages

AUTHOR: V. S. AZARIAH, HENRY WHITEHEAD

Christ in the Indian Villages

By the Right Rev.
V. S. Azariah,
Bishop of Dornakal.

and the Right Rev.
Henry Whitehead,
rmerly Bishop of Madras.

STUDENT CHRISTIAN MOVEMENT PRESS

CHRIST IN THE INDIAN VILLAGES

Christ in the Indian Villages

By

THE RIGHT REV. V. S. AZARIAH, LL.D.

BISHOP OF DORNAKAL

and

THE RT. REV. HENRY WHITEHEAD, D.D.

FORMERLY BISHOP OF MADRAS

STUDENT CHRISTIAN MOVEMENT PRESS

32 RUSSELL SQUARE, LONDON, W.C. 1

CONTENTS

FOREWORD

The object of this book is not to give a complete account of the work of the Church in the villages of India or to discuss fully the many important problems which it involves, but to describe the wonderful manifestation of the presence and power of the Spirit of God in areas where the Church has followed the example of her Master and preached good tidings to the poor, and where the Christian flock has been, in accordance with Christ's command, taught and cared for. Unhappily in some areas this has not been done. Thousands have been admitted into the Church without due preparation and then left as sheep without a shepherd. The results have been disastrous. But we are not concerned with these failures. Our purpose is to make more fully known the great opportunity that lies before the Christian Church to-day in the village districts and to urge that a serious effort should be made to seize the opportunity before it passes away. Hitherto the Church has been ten years behind its opportunities. In view of the new movements that are beginning at the present day, it is of supreme importance that the Church should be awake to the signs of the times and not wait to take action till the door is shut.

V. S. DORNAKAL,
HENRY WHITEHEAD
Bishop.

May 1930.

CHRIST IN THE INDIAN VILLAGES

CHAPTER I

THE IMPORTANCE OF THE VILLAGE

A TOURIST once visited the chief cities of India. He saw the sights that tourists always see and talked to many persons of note. The ablest and most experienced of the British officials in the north said to him: "Would you like to see the most important man in India?" The tourist was delighted. They drove out together into the country and came across a peasant bending his bare back over his primitive plough and twisting the tails of his slow-moving, patient oxen. "That," said the official, "is the most important man in India." He represented the rural folk who form 90 per cent. of the total population and produce the greater part of the wealth of India.

While therefore it is natural for us in England to think of our people in terms of towns and cities, where the majority of the population and the largest share of the wealth are concentrated, in India we need a different outlook. The big industrial centres are few in number. There are hardly a dozen cities with more than a quarter of a million inhabitants and only thirty with 100,000 and upwards. The 750,000 villages are far more important than those thirty towns.

And next to the families they are the most ancient and stable of all the social institutions in India. In earlier ages they were largely self-sufficing and self-governing. Each of the larger villages contained within itself the trades needed to supply the simple wants of its members, farmers, carpenters, weavers, potters, barbers, shop-keepers and money-lenders, Brahman priests to serve the temples of the Hindu gods, and at the other end of the social scale the labourers, sweepers and servants belonging to the despised outcastes. The secular affairs were managed by a headman and a council of five. The village thus lived its own life and managed its own affairs. Owing to the lack of roads and means of transport it was to a large extent isolated and cut off from the world outside.

This independence had its advantages, but when the monsoon rains failed and famine came, no help could be got from outside and the village people simply died by the million; and even at other times the isolation of the village kept it sunk in poverty, ignorance and superstition.

Under the centralized and efficient rule of the British Government and through the influx of Western Civilization this independent, isolated life is becoming a thing of the past. Officials appointed by Government administer the affairs of the village, while railways and motor-cars invade its seclusion and bring it into contact with the world outside. And the schoolmaster is abroad. Rural education is still in its infancy, but there is a school now in about one village in six, and schemes for rural uplift and reconstruction are being devised and started all over India.

A recent report of the Government of India, however, shows how much still needs to be done for the improvement of village life. In the section on rural conditions it says:—

"Even excluding villages on the mountainous and forest-clad confines of India, there are places from which a visit to a doctor would entail a journey of several days, where there is no road more pretentious than a footpath through the fields and where no educated person has ever lived. To such places as these new ideas can hardly penetrate, and agricultural processes, social and religious customs, and superstitions that are almost as old as the race, still exist in full vigour. Even in the bigger and less remote villages conditions are sometimes not much better, for there is still the same lack of contact with progressive ideas, the same lack of educated leadership, the same survival of uneconomic processes and customs. The use of machinery is kept down to the very minimum, and all power required is supplied by the work of men and animals, the latter frequently underfed, undersized and all but useless. There is an immense waste of human time and labour caused by this lack of all but the most primitive and indispensable agricultural implements, a waste which reacts in many more ways than those immediately obvious.

Again, India supports large numbers of diseased and useless cattle which may not be slaughtered or otherwise suitably dealt with because of religious objections, and yet the annual cost of supporting this vast multitude must be enormous.

"The life of the average Indian agriculturist tends to revolve in a vicious circle. After generations of arrested progress he has frequently lost even the desire for improvement and in any case his poverty makes it impossible to grapple with his circumstances. He has not the knowledge and the education to make the best of his resources, and custom holds him in an iron grip. He will borrow from the money-lender at ruinous interest to perform the various ceremonies demanded by religion or social custom, some of them, like funeral ceremonies, occurring all the oftener by reason of the insanitary conditions of his surroundings, the lack of available medical assistance and, often, his poor stamina. Endemic sicknesses like malaria and hookworm, the incidence of which could be greatly reduced if only the villagers had the knowledge and the will to apply themselves to the task, weaken him and affect his work in the fields and consequently lessen the return from his labour."[1]

It is, then, a matter for profound thankfulness, that the Christian Church during the last seventy years has won its most signal triumphs in the

[1] *Report of India in* 1926-27. A statement prepared for presentation to Parliament.

villages of India where the need of regeneration is so urgent and the situation apparently so hopeless. In the following pages we have given a brief account, drawn mainly from our own experience, of the wonderful work that the gospel of Christ is doing in some of the rural areas by bringing to this stagnant mass of poverty and ignorance a new spiritual power and setting millions even of the poorest and most degraded of the village people on the path of progress towards a higher and happier life. Our Lord Jesus Christ said, "I came that they might have life and have it more abundantly." That promise we see now fulfilled in the villages of India.

CHAPTER II

CHRIST AMONG THE OUTCASTES

For the last seventy years the Church of Christ has grown with great rapidity in India. About 1860, after the Mutiny when the Government had passed from the East India Company to the Crown, this rapid spread of Christianity began. There were at that time about a million Indian Christians. Nearly a third of them belonged to the old Syrian church on the Malabar coast, that claims to have been established by the Apostle S. Thomas. Nearly two-thirds were Roman Catholics, the fruit of three and a half centuries of Missionary effort, and a few were connected with various Protestant churches. But during the last seventy years the million Indian Christians have increased to about five millions. In some areas the progress has been startling. In the Telugu country of South India there were in 1880 about 80,000 Telugu Christians, to-day there are about 850,000. In the United Provinces the Indian Christian community increased over 300 per cent. in forty years. In the Punjab between 1881 and 1921 it grew from 6000 to 315,000.

And this rapid increase in numbers has taken place entirely in the villages. Of the 5,000,000 Christians it is estimated that about 93 per cent.

live in the villages. The large majority of these village Christians have come either from the outcastes of Hindu society or from the aboriginal tribes. The Anglican church is in this respect fairly typical of the whole Indian Christian community. It numbers among its members about 500,000 Indians, and of these about 450,000 live in villages. And of those in the villages about 280,000 have come from the outcastes and 50,000 from aboriginal tribes.

The Church in India, therefore, is essentially a village Church. Its problems are village problems, its education needs to be adapted to the conditions of village life and its leaders must be men and women able and willing to live and work among village folk. And it is the Church of the poor. This fact has often been cast in its teeth as a reproach. In reality it is its glory. Psalmists and Prophets in the Jewish church proclaimed that Jehovah is a God who cares for the poor. The Son of God, when he came into the world, was anointed to preach good tidings to the poor. The crowning proof of His Messiahship was that the poor had the gospel preached to them.

What we see, therefore, in India is only one more illustration of a truth, fundamental in the revelation of God's will and character given through Jesus Christ. Throughout the whole course of the history of His Church God has always chosen the foolish things of the world to put to shame the wise, the weak things to put to shame the things that are mighty and the base things and the things that are despised to bring to nought the things that are highly esteemed.

The outcastes of Hindu society are the last people that human judgment would have chosen as material for the building of a Church that is to be God's instrument for converting to faith in Christ the races of India, with their rich heritage of religious thought and philosophy and their ancient culture and civilization. The total number of these outcastes is about sixty millions. The majority are agricultural labourers, and in the towns and villages they are the scavengers, servants and leather workers, doing all the work that is regarded, according to Hindu ideas, as defiling and degrading. They are miserably poor. It has been calculated that the average wage of an outcaste agricultural labourer in South and West India is about two shillings a week. But what has degraded the outcastes more than anything else is the fact that the Hindu religion brands them as untouchable. If a caste man touches an outcaste it is a sin, which has to be atoned for by religious ceremonies; and because the outcastes are untouchable they are not allowed to use the village wells or the main streets of the villages, or to send their children to the public schools. In some parts of South India they are not only untouchable, but unapproachable. They may not come within forty yards of a man or woman belonging to one of the castes above them. A typical Travancore outcaste on the Malabar coast, in the south-west, has been described as " the picture of servile fear "; and a visitor to

Malabar, describing his experiences among some of the outcastes in these parts, said that "the shrinking fear was so abject and the cries of miserable fright were so piteous," that he dared not approach the wretched hovels in which they lived, though he was bent on an errand of mercy.

An enlightened Indian Prince, himself a Hindu by religion, the ruler of a Native State in West India, gave the following account of the position of the outcastes.

"Our depressed classes stand in a position which has nothing parallel or analogous to it in the history of mankind. Slavery is the worst form of injustice which humanity all the world over has known. But the implications of untouchability, to which we in India have condemned a large section of our fellow-men, are in some respects worse than the worst form of slavery. We treat them as no one ought to treat any being, much less a human being. They are made to live outside the village, in an out-of-the-way-corner which is the dirtiest and filthiest part of the village, such as the most degraded of the caste Hindus would never dream of living in. They are not to come within the limits of the temples of the gods, which are the common gods of all the Hindu community. They are not to draw water from the public wells of the villages. They are not to enjoy the benefits of the public rest-houses. They may die of thirst, but they cannot touch the tank or pond of the village. Even for service of the lowest kind they are not to enter the Hindu household. Their very touch is a sin to be avoided at all costs, and to be expiated by washing your body and the clothes covering it."[1]

The late Mr Gokhale, the ablest statesman that India has produced during the last century, spoke about the treatment of the depressed classes as follows:—

"I think all fair-minded persons will have to admit that it is absolutely monstrous that a class of human beings, with bodies similar to our own, with brains that can think and with hearts that can feel, should be perpetually condemned to a low life of utter wretchedness, servitude and mental and moral degradation, and that permanent barriers should be placed in their way so that it should be impossible for them ever to overcome them and improve their lot. This is deeply revolting to our sense of justice. I believe one has only to put oneself mentally into their place to realize how grievous this injustice is. We may touch a cat, we may touch a dog, we may touch any other animal, but the touch of these human beings is pollution! And so complete is now the mental degradation of these people that they themselves see nothing in such treatment to resent, that they acquiesce in it as though nothing better was their due."[2]

A visitor to Travancore says: "I was walking down a road one evening on the south-west coast

[1] *Memoirs of the Maharajah of Kolhalpur*, vol. II, p. 484.

[2] See *Speeches by G. K. Gokhale*, pp. 898-9. Published by G. A. Natesan, Madras.

of India and a Brahman priest, a member of the highest caste, was behind me. Turning a corner I came across about twenty outcastes, coming in from their work in the fields. As soon as they caught sight of the Brahman they scattered about thirty or forty yards on each side of the road, cowered down in abject, servile fear in the mud and slush of the rice fields, put their hands to their mouths, lest their breath should defile the high-caste man, and cried out in harsh, pathetic tones, 'Unclean, unclean,' to give warning of the pollution of their presence."

A British official of long experience in Central India wrote recently: "I have received a petition from the Chamars of a village praying me to record in the village-customs paper their right to the undigested grain which they wash from the droppings of the bullocks which tread the threshing floors. They spread the dung on a slope, pour water over it and the grain is left high and dry like nuggets." This single instance will illustrate the depths of poverty to which these people have been reduced in some parts of India by the tyranny of their fellow-men.

Added to the tyranny of their fellow-men is the paralysing influence of their religion, a crude form of Animism. It is a religion of fear. The outcastes are, if possible, even more depressed and degraded by the terror inspired by their religion than by the fear of man. They believe that the world in which they live is peopled by a multitude of demons, who are the causes of all unusual events, especially of diseases and disasters. These demons surround their villages and are quick to take offence and inflict cholera, smallpox, fever, cattle disease and misfortunes of all kinds on the unhappy villagers. They lurk everywhere, on the tops of palmyra trees, in caves and rocks, in ravines and chasms. They fly about in the air, like birds of prey, ready to pounce down upon any unprotected victim; and the poor people pass through life in constant dread of these invisible powers. The sole object of their religious rites and sacrifices is to avert their wrath. To the outcastes religion is not a source of hope and consolation, but rather of terror and despair.

What strange material for the building of a Church in any land, more especially in India! And yet these are the people whom God has chosen to be His witnesses. It is estimated that during the last fifty years about 80 per cent. of the converts to Christianity have come from the outcastes in the villages.[1] They have come into the Church not singly or even in families, but in large groups. In some cases as many as 2000 have been baptized in a single day. In the large majority of cases the groups vary in size from 50 to 200. The main centres of these mass movements are the Telugu country, the States of Travancore and Cochin, the Punjab and the United Provinces; but similar movements on a smaller scale have also

[1] See *History of Missions in India*, by Dr Richter. Eng. Trs., p. 233.

been taking place in Tinnevelly and in the northern part of the Bombay Presidency.

The Movement in the Telugu Country

In one district of the Telugu country in South India, which is now included in the diocese of Dornakal, the movement of the outcastes towards Christianity began in 1849 with a man called Venkayya. He could neither read nor write and, like the rest of the outcastes, he feared and worshipped a multitude of evil spirits. Before his conversion he was head of a daring gang of outcaste robbers, who for many years were the terror of the whole district in which they lived. Then his son fell ill. In spite of sacrifices offered to the village goddess the child died and Venkayya was in great sorrow. But just at that time he heard from a member of his gang that a new religion was being preached in the district, which taught that the world was made and ruled by one God, a God of righteousness and love, who so loved men, even the outcastes, that He sent His only Son into the world to die for them. In his grief for his own son this message touched his heart. So he gave up offering sacrifices to evil spirits and said every day a simple prayer that he composed himself. "God, teach me who Thou art, show me where Thou art, help me to find Thee." He offered that prayer earnestly for three years, and apparently no answer came. At last he went one day with some of his friends to a town called Bezwada, on the river

Kistna. It was the time of a Hindu religious festival, when many thousands of pilgrims had gathered there and were bathing in the sacred river to wash away their sins. Venkayya stood on the bank watching them. Suddenly a Brahman priest came up to him and asked why he was not bathing.[1]

Venkayya answered boldly that he did not believe in it. "Are you, then, a Christian?" asked the priest. "I am not, but I want to know God," was Venkayya's answer. Then, strangely enough, this Brahman priest whispered to Venkayya that there was a European, living in a bungalow on the hill close by, who could teach him about God. So Venkayya and his friends went off to the house where Mr Darling, a missionary of the Church of England, was living. At the time when they arrived Mr Darling was praying in his study. He was almost in despair about his work. He had just been preaching to the pilgrims by the river and they had treated his message with indifference. For eight years he had been preaching to the caste people, and in the whole of that district he had not made a single convert. After he had poured out his heart to God, he opened his study door and saw Venkayya and his friends kneeling, with their foreheads to the ground, in prayer before the bungalow. He asked what they wanted. Venkayya with outstretched arms went forward and said: "O, Teacher, we are men without wisdom, we

[1] The outcastes in this part of India are untouchable, but not unapproachable.

have come to see you to learn about God." Mr Darling told them the simple story of Jesus Christ and His love. When he had finished, Venkayya rose to his feet and exclaimed with deep emotion: "This is my God, this is my Saviour, I have long been seeking for Him. Now I have found Him and will serve Him." Soon afterwards Mr Darling went to Venkayya's village and taught the outcastes the gospel story. Their masters bitterly opposed him. But, in spite of opposition and persecution, Venkayya and his family with some other outcastes were in due time baptized. Venkayya himself was an ardent witness for Christ to the end of his life. Even when he was blind, in his old age, he would sit outside his mud hut and tell the passers-by about Jesus Christ. And through his preaching more than 500 people were converted and baptized.

That was the foundation of the Church in the Kistna district eighty years ago. In 1918 there were 43,500 Christian adherents of the Church of England in that one district, and in 1928 the numbers had increased to 122,500.

In May 1929 the annual evangelistic campaign was held in that area. About 4000 Christians took part in it. They bore their simple witness to Christ in nearly 1000 villages, and over 125,000 non-Christians listened intently as they told the story of the crucified Saviour. Among their hearers were about 3000 Mahommedans and 62,000 caste people. One caste woman, who owned a considerable amount of property, lent her cart to the outcaste Christian women, and went with them herself, exhorting the caste people to accept Christianity. Other caste people offered money, grain and fruits and cleared the ground for the preachers. As a result of this campaign about 1000 caste people gave in their names to be prepared for baptism, in addition to 2300 outcastes.

The Movement in the Punjab

Equally remarkable is the account of the great movement in the Punjab, which started with the baptism of an outcaste of the despised Chuhra tribe in 1873. His name was Ditt, "a dark little man, lame of one leg," who made a scanty living by buying and selling hides. He heard of Christ from a Christian man of higher social position, but "a weak brother," and he determined to become a Christian. So he walked thirty miles to Sialkot, went to the Rev. S. Martin, a Scottish Presbyterian missionary, and asked to be baptized and allowed to go back to his own people. Mr Martin hesitated. It seemed a risky thing to baptize an outcaste and then send him away with very little knowledge to live isolated from all Church life or Christian fellowship among non-Christian relations and friends. However, just at this time it became necessary for Mr Martin, who had been suffering from fever, to go to the hills. But what was to become of Ditt? To leave this outcaste at the mission station in the care of high-caste workers, was a doubtful course to pursue. To take him to the hills was out of the question. A decision was soon made. Mr Martin baptized Ditt and sent him home to his own village with instructions to share his knowledge with his people.

Ditt had five brothers and the whole family numbered about sixty persons. At first they bitterly resented Ditt's lapse from the religion of the clan. They abused him as a man "without religion," and threatened to excommunicate him from their society. "One of your legs is broken, so may it be with the other," exclaimed an angry sister-in-law.

Ditt met their taunts and curses meekly, but unmoved. "You may attack me and abuse me, but you will never induce me to deny Christ." In three months he had the great joy of bringing to faith in the Saviour his wife and daughter and two of his neighbours. He taught them as well as he could and then walked with them the thirty miles to Sialkot and presented them to Mr Martin, who baptized them, and sent them back with Ditt to be witnesses to Christ among their own people. Six months later Ditt brought four more of his neighbours for baptism.

From this small beginning, like a grain of mustard seed, the Presbyterian Church in that district has sprung up with marvellous rapidity, spreading from home to home and village to village. Almost every new convert became an evangelist, telling the good news of the Kingdom of God. To-day the United Presbyterian Church in the Punjab has a Christian community numbering 85,000, of whom

24,000 are communicants. And over fifty of the congregations support their own pastors.

In the same area of the Punjab there are also 40,000 Anglican Christians drawn from the outcastes connected with the Church Missionary Society, and an equal number who are members of the Roman Catholic Church and the Salvation Army.

In the whole of India, as a result of these mass movements among the outcastes, during the last fifty years nearly 2,000,000 people have been gathered into the Church of Christ.

CHAPTER III

MIGHTY WORKS

THE mighty works of Jesus Christ during His ministry, the healing of the sick and the casting out of devils, were signs to the Jewish people that the Kingdom of God had come upon them.[1]

The preaching of the Apostles after the day of Pentecost was confirmed by similar signs and wonders, and by a striking transformation of life and character within the Christian community.[2]

The same is true of the work of the Christian Church in the villages of India. Devils are cast out, men and women are turned from the worship of demons to the worship of the one true God, thousands and tens of thousands are converted from sin to righteousness, and the lives of whole communities are transformed. God bears witness to the message of salvation "both with signs and wonders and with divers miracles, and gifts of the Holy Ghost according to his own will." [3]

It is true that the motives that lead people to become Christians in mass movements in the villages are often strangely mixed. Some become Christians because others do. The herd instinct is strong in

[1] See Matt. xii. 28; Acts ii. 22.
[2] See Acts ii. 43 ff.; iv. 8 ff., 21; v. 14 ff.; viii. 6,7; xiv. 3.
[3] See Hebrews ii. 3-4.

India. In one village where large numbers gave in their names to be prepared for baptism, they were asked why they wanted to join the Church. Several reasons were given, among others the desire for self-improvement and for the education of their children. "There is no school in this village," said one man, "all these children tend cattle and grow like asses." Another said, "We are tired of worshipping these idols; they are no good." In another village a group of new converts gave as their reason for becoming Christians: "Because we were bad and wanted to become better"; and that probably sums up the feeling that leads the majority to join the Church. In a very real sense they long for salvation from a bad, degrading life, and see that large numbers of their own community have found it in this new religion.

Providential and supernatural reasons are sometimes assigned, too, as immediate occasions for accepting Christianity. There was a man who had been a Hindu devotee and priest and a hater of Christians. While still a boy he had become an orphan and had been brought up by an old Christian aunt for whom he had great regard. Her one grief in her old age was that this nephew was such an unbending Hindu. The man was a devout worshipper of the village goddess Gangamma. Every Saturday he fasted, and early on Sunday he broke his fast after making a meal offering at the shrine of Gangamma. One night he dreamt a dream. He saw some grand personage approaching him and taking tight hold of his arm. He heard the command: "Go to the Christian Church." He woke, but thought no more of it and continued as usual. This was on a new moon night. On the next new moon night this dream was repeated. Still he disregarded it. The dream was repeated on the third new moon night; and the august person would not loose his grip until the man gave him a solemn promise. He yielded, but wanted three weeks' respite. He went to the chapel a week before the next new moon day. He was converted: he gave up worshipping Gangamma and became a most regular worshipper in the Christian Church at daily prayers. In due course he was baptized and later was confirmed and is now a most faithful communicant and a keen witness to the living presence and power of the Lord.

Then, there are many who come out because in Christ they find rest from their evil past. "We were tired of that life of drink and robbery and we knew that our only hope was in this religion," is a familiar answer. "In what ways are you different now from what you were before?" was asked of a man of a robber caste. "Are we not different?" came the ready reply, "men and women go to prayer every night; we do not now commit burglary; we do not drink; we enjoy heaven now: we were in hell before."

But what gives such a wonderful moral power to the movement, is the simple faith in the Fatherhood of God and the saving power of Jesus Christ that inspires the majority of the Christians. Nothing else but the power of the Spirit of Christ could have produced the transformation that has taken place on a vast scale in their lives. Dr Stanley Jones tells us that at a meeting of educated Hindus he once said: "Brothers, what can we do with those outcastes? They are a millstone around our national neck. Our country will never be strong until we lift them. How can we do it?" A thoughtful Hindu arose and said, "It will take a Christ to lift them." And that is true.

The accounts given by missionaries working among the outcastes in different parts of India during the last fifty years are full of stories that illustrate this saving power of Christ. The courage and steadfastness of new converts under persecution is itself very wonderful, when we consider how little they know and how brief is their experience of Christ. It has been often said that these poor people easily become Christians because they have everything to gain and nothing to lose by it. From a worldly point of view that is often very far from the truth. When the outcastes of a village first join the Christian Church, especially in the early days of a movement, they are often subjected to bitter and cruel persecution by their Hindu masters; they are beaten, deprived of their land and cattle, if they have any, false charges are brought against them and they are thrown into prison. Yet they stand firm.

A missionary in the United Provinces gives an account of a small band of inquirers in a village who were persecuted in various ways by their master. "Give up Christianity," he said, "and I will stop persecuting you." "No," was their reply, "imprison us; hang us if you like; *but we have taken hold of God and we are not letting go.*"[1] A year afterwards they were baptized with great rejoicing.

One of the C.M.S. missionaries in the Telugu Mission tells the story of one man who came to him with his right hand terribly burned. When he announced his intention of becoming a Christian the headman in his village called upon him to renounce Christianity. When he refused, the headman threatened to put his right hand into boiling oil. As he still stood firm, the threat was carried out, and he came to the missionary, having nobly stood fast under that trial, with his right hand charred and withered and utterly useless.

In another district an old man was baptized with the appropriate name of Job. When he said he was going to become a Christian the headman of his village took away his cattle; when he persevered, he took away his land. Then the old man came to be baptized, rejoicing that he had been thought worthy to suffer the loss of all things for the sake of Christ.

The people in another village were asked whether they knew of anyone completely changed by becoming a Christian. One man replied: "Yesuratnam in our village was a man like that. The caste people asked him to offer as usual the sacrifice at the boundary festival and kill a chicken and pour

[1] C.M.S. Mass Movement Quarterly, March 1927 and March 1928.

the blood on cooked rice, and then carry the blood-sprinkled rice round the boundaries of the land, to invoke the blessing of the goddess on the crop. Yesuratnam refused to do this because he was a Christian. They threatened to withhold all wages, and gathered round him with sticks and threatened to beat him if he was obstinate. Yesuratnam explained that as a Christian he could carry neither the rice nor the blood, nor offer the sacrifice; but he would walk round the boundaries of the land and pray to the Lord Jesus for a good harvest. They permitted him to do as he suggested. Since then, the caste people respect our religion."

A woman added: "There is one in our village also, Samuel. He gave up drink himself, made the whole village give up drink, then fought with the Sudras to get the liquor shop removed from the village. The Hindus afterwards acknowledged that Christianity was a good religion."

The power of Christ to save is often manifested, as in the case of Venkayya,[1] among the criminal classes. The following is an illustration.

Lakshikadu was a Yerukala, and did not belong to the outcastes. He was a caste man—his touch was not pollution. He could live near the caste quarters, he could take water from the caste people's well. The occupation of this caste was basket-making, mat-weaving, fortune-telling, house-breaking and highway robbery. His father died when he was only six months old and his mother brought him up by hard work. Lakshikadu was

[1] See Chapter II.

sixteen years old when four Yerukalas happened to spend two days at his hut feasting and drinking. When they left, they took the boy with them to a neighbouring village where they had planned a robbery. His daring spirit soon won their confidence and he became a regular member of the gang and took part in many robberies. It was an exciting life as long as it lasted: but the plunder was all spent in drink and riotous living and there were, of course, regular intervals of poverty and starvation. At last Lakshikadu was caught by the police and sentenced to two months' imprisonment; but in spite of severe pressure he stedfastly refused to betray his comrades. On his release he took to the forest and became a noted dacoit.

A body of police was deputed to track him down and one of them found him seated on a rock in the heart of the forest. Lakshikadu seeing this man, slowly climbed down on the other side, but left his large turban on the summit of the rock. The policeman fired and brought the turban down. When he ran up to seize his man, Lakshikadu sprang upon him and tied him to a tree with his own turban, broke his rifle and decamped. However, he was caught in the end and imprisoned for six months. On his leaving the prison, he spent a night at a police station, where he met a Christian police inspector who advised him to give up his lawless life and become a Christian. When he went back to his home he found that his wife had come under the influence of one of the Indian missionaries of the Dornakal Mission.

She begged him to go with her and hear the preaching. For some time he refused in spite of her importunity, but at last she adopted the method of non-co-operation, and declined to cook or eat anything till he went. This brought matters to a crisis and he gave way and began to attend Christian prayers. He gave up drinking, learnt carpentry and began to learn Telugu letters so that he might read the Bible. After some months he and his wife were baptized and took the names, Thomas and Prema (love).

All was not over yet. His caste pride would not let him present himself for confirmation, which, he knew, would be followed by Holy Communion, and he was not yet prepared to have communion with the outcaste converts. After a year the husband and wife came and wanted to be confirmed. They said they had thought over it and came to the conclusion that there was no pollution in partaking of " the sacred food." It took another three years before they could reconcile themselves to make no distinction in social life. It was a hard struggle. At one time Prema said, " I know it is not right, but I cannot bring my mind to sit down to the same meal with these people. But I am praying that God may remove this feeling from our hearts." Even this was overcome later on, and Thomas and Prema have often been seen seated between Mala and Madiga converts and enjoying a wedding feast. Thomas has forgotten his old life, earns his livelihood by carpentry and freely witnesses to the power of Jesus Christ.

His wife is a Bible teacher and has a very good working knowledge of the Bible. When the police saw the change in his life, they recommended that he be exempted from police surveillance. He can now go anywhere without a pass. He is a member of the Parish committee and the local Church Council and both Thomas and Prema are respected and loved by everybody in Dornakal.

In many similar cases true conversion comes long after baptism, not infrequently at confirmation. Joseph belongs to one of the outcaste communities. He had been a great drunkard and thief. He continued to be so even after his baptism. He did not become a Christian from any religious motive. He "joined the religion" and was baptized; he came up for confirmation, because everybody in the village was doing so. But then came the change. Two years after his confirmation he narrated his experiences:—

"Four years ago I joined the religion when our whole village came over. I had been a great drunkard. I was in a gang who also occasionally committed burglary; there is hardly a crime or sin that I have not been guilty of. We came very near to murder sometimes. When all the others in the village became Christians I became a Christian too; but I did not give up any of my bad ways. We did give up idolatry and the worship of the old gods and goddesses. But that was all. The whole village was prepared for baptism, so was I and we were all baptized together. But even after baptism I continued to drink, to rob and to steal. Once my comrades and I succeeded in removing our Christian teacher's cow from his house and led it many miles to a far off village over night and slaughtered it for meat before daybreak and returned to our village in the morning. When confirmation classes were held I also joined, but had not realized what it meant. But I began to feel very bad: I thought I was unworthy to receive the blessing of the Holy Spirit; and yet I kept on. On the day appointed for the confirmation the candidates of our village arrived late and we were all, therefore, seated last. I was glad of it, because I felt myself unworthy of confirmation. We listened to the examination and address; but I was inwardly feeling very bad. I felt that I did not deserve to go up to be confirmed. When the time came, the pastor came to the last row and we stood up and I, who was sitting last, was made to go first. This was too much for me! I had been feeling that I deserved no blessing at all: I was certainly the greatest sinner in the crowd: to go last after all the rest might be suitable, but to go first, I was not ready! But I could not refuse; I had to go. Tears were running down my eyes, as I thought what a wicked life I had led these many years. After confirmation I went back to my seat, knelt down and then and there gave myself to be a new man. I said, 'O God, Thy love to me the greatest of sinners is something I cannot bear. For the sake of Jesus Christ who died for me forgive me! Hereafter I shall be a different man. Give me the strength and power of the Holy Spirit to live for Thee.' Instantly a great joy came over me and I felt a different man. I went home and nothing happened for a week. Then came the harvest and my landlord made a present of a pot of toddy for all the labourers and asked me to distribute it. I said I did not myself drink and so preferred not to have anything to do with it. He laughed. He could not believe me. I told him that ever since our Bishop came I had given up drink. He pointed out that the Bishop was no longer there and there was no harm in drinking or giving others some toddy after a hard day's work. I said I could not do that, because I had vowed before God that I would be a different man. But there was another difficulty. My annual wage was Rs. 36 (£2, 14s.) in cash, and about another Rs. 36 in grain. This had been sufficient because I made up the deficiency by stealing grain, vegetables, tobacco and all other supplies from my master's farm. This I could no longer do, with the result that I was falling into debt. I went to my master and said, 'My wages are insufficient and I am falling into debt. Please therefore let me go away so that I may do my own cultivation.' He said, 'What? Do you tell me that after all those years your wages have become insufficient all of a sudden?' I said that was what I meant, and asked him whether he really thought we were all living on the wages he was giving us. I explained how all the vegetables for our use came from his garden, all the tobacco we used was from his store, how

I always brought home without his knowledge my share of his grain. But now, I said, I could not do these things and the wages were inadequate. My master laughed and said it was a strange story, though he quite believed it."

The master wanted time to consider his request, and for a month he carefully watched him at work, but at the end of the month he made him his head labourer and doubled his wages.

The teacher in charge of one village told the following story: "Four years ago Abraham was known to be the most wild and quarrelsome man in my village. He was an habitual drunkard. When the Deanery chairman came to the village for the Harvest festival, I went to Abraham's house to call him to the service. He said he would come later. Again I went; he was not at home; he had gone to the liquor shop. I went to it and there was Abraham, very drunk and challenging every one to fight. I came away very sad. Four months later there was a confirmation for our Pastorate. Four candidates were ready from my village. Abraham wanted to go too. As he did not know any confirmation lessons, I left him behind. After the Bishop's examination of the candidates was finished Abraham appeared in the chapel and sat down with the others, without my seeing him. So by mistake he was confirmed. After we had all returned to the village, a radical change was noticed in Abraham. He never touched drink, he was the first to come to Church services. That was three years ago. This year he has been elected by the congregation to be their representative on the church council." The teacher was asked, "What do you think effected the change?" "Nothing but the grace of the Holy Spirit," was his reply.

But the most impressive fact about this movement is the fuller and more abundant life, intellectual, moral and spiritual, that comes to the Christian community as a whole through the liberty of the Spirit. We see the same thing happening in India to-day that happened seventeen centuries ago in the Roman Empire. Dr Glover points out that Christianity triumphed in the ancient world "because essentially it liberated the human mind and gave it a chance to develop to the full range of God's conception of it."[1]

In this respect the parallel between the Church in the Roman and that in the Indian Empire is amazingly close: in both cases "not many wise after the flesh, not many mighty, not many noble are called,"[2] and in both cases there is the same wonderful "liberation of the human mind." When we consider the oppression, the degradation and the starvation of body and soul to which the outcastes have been subjected for more than a thousand years we should naturally expect that it would need many generations of teaching and culture to raise them up to the intellectual and cultural level of their masters. But that is very far from the truth. In the second generation the

[1] *The Influence of Christ in the Ancient World*, pp. 9, 10. By T. R. Glover (Cambridge) University Press, 1929.

[2] 1 Cor. i. 26.

transformation often is startling. A small outcaste boy, whose parents were Christians, was taken by one of the missionaries to the Telugu country and started by pulling the punkahs in the missionary's bungalow. He was sent to the mission school and is now an able Wesleyan minister, greatly respected by Christians and Hindus alike over a large district, doing with singular wisdom and patience a most valuable work of rural uplift.

Another Tamil outcaste boy, minding cattle in the fields for a few pence a week, attended the primary classes of a mission school, rose in time to be one of the leading ministers in the Congregational Church of South India, mayor of the town in which he lived and a leader in the great movement towards Church unity in South India. At the beginning of 1929 he died, and at his funeral there was a remarkable demonstration of respect and affection from all classes, Europeans and Indians, Christians, Hindus and Moslems. The shops were closed and the leading men of the town attended the funeral service. In the whole of South India there are more than 200 ministers and priests drawn from the outcastes; and in the village districts, where they work, they stand head and shoulders above the mass of caste Hindus in education, character and spiritual life.

In one of the Anglican stations in the Telugu country there is a High School in which for the last thirty years there has been approximately an equal number of pupils drawn respectively from the outcaste Christians and the high-caste Hindus. If a comparison were made of the number of students from each of these two sections that have passed the final High School examination, conducted by the Government Education Department during the last thirty years, it would be found that there was no great difference between the outcaste Christians and the high-caste Hindus.

Recently a Baptist missionary gave a remarkable illustration of this liberation of the spirit in a family connected with his mission. A Madiga Christian woman, belonging to the lowest section of the outcastes, married a low-caste convert. They had two sons. One is now a professor in a University college and the other is a learned Telugu scholar.

The effect of this new liberty, that is the gift of the Spirit of Christ, is even more striking among the women than among the men. A poor Madiga girl, whose mother would not have been allowed to touch the children of caste Hindus or even to be in the same room with them, is now the head-mistress of a large girls' school attended by the children of both high-caste Hindus and well-to-do Mahommedans. In another school of this kind every single teacher is a Christian girl of outcaste origin. In December 1929, after the baptism of a large number of converts in a village in the Dornakal diocese, some of the leading men from the Caste quarter of the village, which has a population of about 3000, asked that a Christian girl might be sent to take charge of a school for their girls. And a Christian girl in that district would necessarily be an outcaste.

In the large town of Bezwada in the Telugu country, when a municipal election was recently held, a number of educated women were needed to instruct the illiterate female voters how to fill up their voting-papers. The only women available were Christians.

And still more striking than these individual instances is the outburst of song and drama that has swept over the large Christian community in the Telugu country during the last few years. Christian songs and lyrics are composed by large numbers of people and sung to Telugu tunes. The women and children especially sing them with great delight by the hour together. Musical dramas are being composed on various subjects, such as the life and message of the prophets Amos and Jeremiah, the life and work of St Paul and the history of Joseph. One of the most recent is on the life of Venkayya, whose story is given above.

During the annual Health Week at Dornakal the final item of the programme is a musical health drama composed by the school teachers and acted by the children. These dramas are extraordinarily effective for their purpose. Large audiences are held spell-bound for hours and receive an immense amount of useful teaching. During one of these weeks last year, men and women eagerly bought and read 1500 booklets on sanitation, precautions against smallpox and cholera, and on other subjects connected with health. No doubt they begin at a low level in these matters, but the significant fact is that they have the desire and courage to start on the upward path.

CHAPTER IV

THE TRANSFORMATION OF VILLAGES [1]

CHRISTIANITY is a social religion. It not only aims at bringing individual souls under the regenerating influence of Jesus Christ, but it also unites the disciples of Christ in a society and makes that society the instrument for carrying out God's purpose in the world. The testimony of the individual is effective, but the testimony of the society is even more powerful. What then is the effect of the Gospel on the Christian community? The following incident will serve to illustrate this in a village where the people became Christians after much hesitation. They were not at first particularly strong in the faith. They are typical of a large number of Christian communities in the Telugu country.

We were camping in the Traveller's Bungalow. I finished the Confirmation one evening, and had a service of Holy Communion in the morning with the workers and those of the newly confirmed who stayed over night for it. It was soon found that nobody in the village itself was a Christian. I was told that the antagonistic attitude of the Dorai—the landlord who belonged to a leading Zamindari

[1] This chapter is by the Bishop of Dornakal.

family of the district—made any movement impossible. My wife and I wanted to visit the Dorai's house and so started out when the sun was fairly down, and on the way visited the outcaste village. After seeing the Dorai we returned to the Bungalow, and were at dinner, when I noticed a crowd outside. I went out and found about twenty men, mostly young, and asked them who they were.

"We belong to Kondur," came the reply. "Did you not, with 'Amma Garu'[1] come to our village this evening?"

"Oh, yes," I said, "What do you want?"

"We have come to tell you that we want to join the religion."

"What!" I said. "You did not seem to be very keen in the afternoon; what is it that has produced this change of mind now?"

"After you and the Amma Garu left us, we began to consult together; and later, when all the elders came home from the fields we summoned a meeting of the whole village, and we decided that we must become Christians now. We want to do it at once because the Bishop has come to our village."

"That sounds very nice; but *why* do you want to become Christians?"

"For some years we have wanted to become Christians; and we enrolled ourselves once before; but as soon as our landlord heard of it he placed difficulties in our way and we could not stand the persecutions. But now, we see that all the villages

[1] Lady Mother.

round about us have joined the religion and they are all going ahead in every way and we alone are left behind. Soon we shall be unable even to get brides and bridegrooms for our children unless we become Christians."

"But the Dorai will again persecute you," I said.

"Let him; we shall all leave the village and go elsewhere: but we want the religion, we are not going to give it up this time even if our throats are cut."

The Pastor and Mr Adam, the Indian Rural Dean, one of our most trusted Indian leaders, were in another part of the Bungalow and I sent for the latter. He came and I repeated the whole conversation to him. He was very pessimistic.

"You talk like this now," said he to the deputation, "but when the Dorai finds this out, he will beat you, threaten to drive you out of the village and then you will yield to his threats. I can't believe your words."

"No, no, sir," they said. "We are not going to do that. Let him beat us, let him drive us out of the village, let him cut our throats. We are not going back this time."

Mr Adam: "If this is true, will you have your tufts removed now?[1] Then I will believe you are sincere."

[1] Removing the tuft is in certain parts of the Telugu country considered a distinctive outward badge of having left the Hindu Society and joined the Christian Society. In old days the tuft of hair on the top of the head was identified with adherence to the Hindu faith.

The elders demurred. They were of course taken aback at this unforeseen challenge. The hour was late; it would be inconvenient to go and have a bath or to wash their hair after the operation. My wife, noticing the struggle, pleaded that this ceremony might be left over till the morning.

"No, no," said the young men. "It must be done now. If we are allowed to go away now, we might find it difficult to make the decision later!" So they all agreed, sat down, untied the knots and let down their long hair, ready for the scissors. My nail scissors were the only pair we had. Mr Adam took charge of them: the bungalow peon, who was a Roman Catholic caste man, held up the lantern, and then and there about twenty of them had their tufts removed and thus broke with the past.

"When the landlord sees you in the morning and notices the tufts gone, then will come trouble," Mr Adam said.

"Come what may," was the chorus of reply. They had broken with the past: they were ready for anything. We knelt on that verandah and committed the village to the grace of God.

Next evening at nine o'clock was to be the first service, when the names were to be enrolled. We all went. The men whose tufts had not been removed the previous night had "to be done" now. Then all the names were taken down—one hundred and fifty-one in all.

The elder said: "Iyah (sir), we have a request to make."

"Yes, go on!"

"Do you know Teacher Sanjeevi of——? That is the teacher we want. He teaches well. The people improve quickly under him. The children love him. We have seen it. Will you not please give us that teacher?"

"But you must find a house for him, you must put up a school building; not until then can the teacher come!" was Mr Adam's reply.

"We shall have the house ready to-morrow! We have a thatched shed now in the centre of the village used for common village meetings. That can be used as chapel and school. Can the teacher come to-morrow?"

So we decided to effect the change. Money? We did not know whether there was money or not. But people with such keenness could not be left unprovided for. So Mr Adam said he would send the teacher at once and take the chances. Then we had prayers. I spoke to them about prayer—that God was our Father and as children tell their fathers all their needs, they must learn to tell the Heavenly Father all they needed—that they could pray always and everywhere—in the fields, in the houses, the last thing at night and first thing in the morning and so forth. And we knelt to pray.

They had taken the first step. They had so far given the Spirit of God room to begin His regenerating work in their souls. The seed had been sown. It was sure to do its work. We left them on the following day. That was in October 1924. They were baptized a year later in September 1925.

The first sixty-five of the adults were confirmed in February 1927. The first communion was held on the following morning in a mud chapel that the people had built for themselves. It was not quite finished. The roof was on. The walls were only half up. Two windows were in position. We had the celebration there in this place made sacred by loving devotion. I could hardly recognize the faces of the people: they had all so altered! Their cleanliness, order, their devotion and their loving adoration—who could tell they were the same people that met me on that October night in 1924? As I described the meaning of the Sacrament they were now to receive their faces shone. They had realized what the Cross of Christ had meant to them. They had seen its transforming power. The teaching during these two years had centred round the Cross. God so loved us and gave Himself for us! It was a wonderful service. God was near. The Spirit was moving us. As the women came and put out their hands to receive the Sacrament, their eyes were wet with tears!

Late in the evening a messenger came saying that the Dorai was coming to visit us. We got some chairs in position and were ready to receive him. He gave us limes, salaamed us both, placed a big dish of fruit in front of us—said it was for *amma garu*, and excused himself that he had not better fruit. I began: "How are you? How is the family? Since we were here last time, these villagers have become Christians; what do you think of their new religion?"

"Iyah"(sir), came the ready reply, "that is what brought me here now. I wanted to come to thank you for this religion. I never realized that Christianity was such a religion. You have seen the people now. How they have changed! They are clean, all their foul speech has gone! Their singing, their worship, their devotion is a marvel to us! They are honest, they give us better work. We are all pleased about this religion. The teacher—ah! He is a good man! Though he comes from the outcastes, he can come into my house now. He is our family physician. I want to write to all the Zamindars and dorais that no one should hinder this religion entering any of their villages. If it were possible we should all become Christians."

And this was the man of whom they were afraid; as a man who might even cut their throats!

The impression thus made upon the caste people by the transformation of outcaste communities in their own villages is the strongest possible evidence of the spiritual power of the gospel of Christ. And it is very widespread.

In a village in a remote part of the Hyderabad State about twenty years ago a few outcastes were baptized, the first Christians in the village. They were miserably poor, very dirty and depressed. Later on the whole of the outcastes in the village were converted to Christianity. And in about twelve years there was a miraculous transformation of the whole village. Through the influence of the outcaste Christians and their teacher, the caste people of the village had given up idolatry. The sacrifices to the village gods and goddesses at times of sowing and harvest, that they and their forefathers had offered for thousands of years, were abolished. "We offer our prayers and make our vows to your God only," they said to the Indian pastor. Many of them had given up drunkenness and foul language. "We are ashamed of these things now," they said, "when we see the outcastes living sober and respectable lives." To anyone who knows the strength of caste and the rigid conservatism of the Indian villages this was indeed a miracle.

I was about to hold a Confirmation at the village of B——. After robing, I came out to the temporary palm leaf pavilion erected for the purpose. There were about a hundred people, young and old, arranged on the ground and singing lyrics. There were also seated on benches inside some Hindu caste gentlemen who had come to see the function. I did not like these men to be mere spectators inside the pavilion, and so very courteously I asked them to withdraw until we finished our prayers. They got up at once—but waited a whole hour outside looking on. We met again after the service was over. "What did you think of our service?" I asked. "Oh, sir, that is what we want to tell you. We know these people very well: they are our own servants. Their fathers and forefathers worked for our fathers and forefathers. They are not superior to us in caste, they are not superior to us in wealth, they are not superior to us in education, they are not superior to us in looks: and yet, when we sat and looked at them before you came in, we could not fail to notice the bright rays of the glory of God playing on their faces; we have not got that!"

At K——, the village magistrate (who was a casteman) was observing my examination of the candidates for confirmation, and when the candidates left I asked him to tell me what he really thought of our Christian converts. His reply was this: "I must tell you the truth, I cannot deny that there is a real change among these people since Christianity was introduced among them. Formerly they drank heavily, every decent man shunned their village after sunset—the quarrels and the foul language used were too loathsome for words. Cattle poisoning by these people was common. Now all that has changed. Cattle-poisoning is now unknown in Christian villages. Instead of drunken revels and quarrels, the music of lyrics and songs from the village chapel fill the air in the evenings. In short, these people are learning, nay have learnt, to live soberly, righteously and godly in the villages."

At N——, two caste Reddies, the leaders of one of the villages where we have a congregation, came to see me. They had walked five miles for this purpose. The outcaste people had been Christians for seven years; but they had lived very indifferent lives. During the two years previous to my visit, however, there had been a change in the teacher and in the pastor, and a new life had been introduced into the congregation. This the

Reddy had observed. He said: "Only now we have come to see what Christianity is. This religion has been in our village for seven years; but it produced no impression on us. Since the coming of this new teacher everything has changed. These people have now learnt good manners, they know now how to behave towards us, how to work for us, and even how to talk to us; theft has stopped, we now respect the Christian people, even though they are outcastes: and we respect their religion too."

The importance of having as teachers devout men, trained and equipped for rural work was never more forcibly brought home to me than when this Hindu Reddy gave this testimony. Rural evangelism demands first-class men.

Our largest congregation of Madiga converts is at M——. There are over 800 people in this one place who are members of our church. In its neighbourhood is a large village of well-to-do caste people. The Christians earn their livelihood by working for the caste landowners. Some work on monthly wages: the others get daily wages for tasks connected with rice cultivation. Years ago, when I held my first Confirmation in this village, some of the leading caste men came to witness our service. On questioning them as to what they thought of our worship, they said it was very elevating and they liked the moral teaching we gave the people. I asked them what they thought of our Christians. The reply came from one of the thoughtful men. "We can say," he said, "that these Madigas have learnt real *bhakti* (devotion) since they became Christians." It was a delightful testimony, but I wondered at the time how far it came from real conviction. But quite recently the Christian houses were all destroyed by fire in one night and the condition of the people was most piteous. The houses were all small thatched houses and burnt themselves out in no time. Very little of the meagre belongings of the unfortunate Christians was saved. Without clothes or food they were in a most hopeless position. As soon as the extent of the loss was known, the Hindu gentlemen came most generously with offers of help. One leading man spent about £200 in giving temporary relief in clothes and grain to the Christian sufferers. During these many years respect and regard for these outcaste Christians had grown, until it found expression in such a splendid act of spontaneous generosity.

Non-Christians have not only given an unqualified testimony to the change that has been wrought in outcaste communities by the power of the Gospel of Christ, but in many cases they have themselves entered into a larger life and faith through the example of their Christian servants.

CHAPTER V

A MOVEMENT AMONG THE CASTES

THE conversion of caste people to faith in Christ is no new thing. Members of various castes have for many centuries been converted to faith in Christ in large numbers. The Syrian Christian community on the south-west coast, numbering at present about 800,000, were originally drawn from the caste people in Travancore and Cochin. Large numbers of caste people were also converted first by the Jesuit missionaries from A.D. 1600 onwards, and then by Protestant missionaries in the eighteenth and nineteenth centuries. So that the total number of Christians gathered from the Hindu castes is at present considerably over a million.

One disappointing feature, however, in these movements among the caste people in the past has been their tendency to stagnation. They have started with great spiritual power and then after a time have ceased to progress. That has been the case with the old Syrian church in Travancore and Cochin, and with the caste converts both of the Roman Catholic church and of the Protestant churches in other parts of India. The main reason for this stagnation is the fact that the deep-rooted caste feeling of Hindu society has persisted after conversion and has ultimately prevailed over the spirit of Christian brotherhood. In many parts of South India the Christian community has not only failed to evangelize the depressed classes but has actively opposed their admission to the Christian Church. The same spirit is manifested among many of the more highly educated Christians, drawn from various castes in North India. For social reasons they are definitely opposed to the gathering of the poor and depressed into the Church and regard the mass movements of the outcastes not as an opportunity for service but as a grievous hindrance to the fulfilment of their ambitions.[1]

The inevitable result of this unchristian spirit is a loss of spiritual power. A very learned Brahman convert, Father Nehemiah Goreh, once said that "Christianity with caste is no Christianity at all." Unhappily Christian missionaries in the past have not been sufficiently alive to this deadly peril. The Jesuit missionaries in the seventeenth century made terms with caste and admitted it into the Church and many of the Protestant missionaries followed their example. It seemed the line of least resistance, but it was a fatal blunder. A Roman Catholic missionary in South India recently remarked that they had admitted caste into the Church three centuries ago and bitterly regretted it. "But," he added, "it is now too late, we cannot get rid of it."

[1] See *The Christian Task in India*, pp. 244 ff.; *The Making of Modern India*, pp. 199 ff. Macnicol.

A MOVEMENT AMONG THE CASTES

The new movement among the caste people in the villages of the Telugu country towards Christianity that has been in progress during the last ten or fifteen years is all the more hopeful because it promises to deal effectively from the start with the caste feeling. The movement has been mainly due to the witness of the changed lives of the outcaste Christians and the personal influence of individual teachers and ministers drawn from the outcastes. Previous chapters have described the effect that this witness and influence have had in conciliating prejudice and creating a friendly feeling among the caste people towards Christianity. But within the last ten years this has begun to bear fruit in definite conversions to faith in Christ. Considerably over 10,000 caste people in the Telugu country have already been baptized, and they have joined a church in which more than 800,000 Christians have been drawn from the outcastes. So that in nearly every village where these caste converts exist, they worship with outcaste Christians and are ministered to by outcaste clergy, catechists and teachers! This strikes from the beginning a powerful blow at the caste feeling. And it is noticeable that the higher the caste from which the converts come, the more completely they abandon caste prejudices, when once they have crossed the Rubicon at baptism. It often seems easier for a Brahman convert to eat with an outcaste than for different sections of the outcastes to eat together.

This movement among the caste people is taking place over a very wide area in the Telugu country.

Guntur

In the area where the American Lutheran Church is working with its head-quarters at Guntur it began about twenty years ago in a district where there were already a large number of Roman Catholics, drawn from different castes during the last sixty or seventy years. The beginning of this movement in the Lutheran church was due to the strong personal influence of a Lutheran missionary and his wife working in that district. Many hundreds became Christians, but at first, owing to the influence of the Roman Catholics who had been allowed to keep their caste, there was a serious danger of the caste spirit becoming permanent among them. Caste boarding-schools were established exclusively for caste children and in other ways caste prejudices were respected. Happily this policy was reversed, the schools were thrown open to outcaste and caste alike and the caste Christians learned to accept the ministrations of outcaste ministers and teachers.

Later on the movement started in other districts within the area. It was mainly due to the personal influence of outcaste teachers and their wives, backed by the changed lives of the outcaste congregations; but in a few cases it began with an individual man who was a true seeker after God.

In one village the munsiff (magistrate) was a student of different religions. He studied carefully Hinduism, Buddhism and Mahommedanism and could find no peace or satisfaction. Then he turned to Christianity and the study of the Bible, and after many talks with Lutheran missionaries was convinced of the truth of Christianity. He was finally baptized with about sixty of his friends and relations.

In another village there was a caste man who belonged to the sect of Lingayets and was a follower of the Hindu reformer Ramanuja. A tract was given him one day in a railway train by a lady missionary and this started him on the study of the Bible. He went to Guntur where he was taught by the missionaries and baptized.

Through these various influences the movement spread throughout the area with the result that about 6000 of the caste people have already been baptised.

Dornakal

In the Dornakal diocese the movement has been rapidly growing in strength during the last five years. Sometimes it has been due to the witness of a single outcaste. The following story told by one of the C.M.S. missionaries is an illustration of this.

" When I had been at Bezwada about eighteen months a young Sudra man named Ramayya appeared one day on my verandah with his wife and little boy. He had travelled about eighty miles from his home, a village in the Khammamett District (C.M.S.) in the Nizam's Dominions. He told me that he desired to be taught about Jesus Christ, having learnt about him first from a certain old Christian named Abraham (a convert from the outcastes) who was employed by his (Ramayya's) father. Abraham had evidently taught the young Sudra some of the salient facts about our Lord and a few lyrics, and had passed away. But his witness had sown seed in the heart of Ramayya, who, no longer able to learn from his old friend, determined to seek further light from the mission to which Abraham belonged. Fearing to go to the mission station nearest his village, namely Khammamett, lest his relations should discover his intentions and bring him back, he came to Bezwada on the plea of wishing to visit some relatives near there. I received Ramayya, his wife and child, and gladly arranged for them to be housed and given regular instruction in my compound. But I advised him to let me send news of him to his relatives. There proved to be no need for this, however, for the next day a crowd of his relatives turned up, having somehow discovered Ramayya's real object in leaving home. They tried their utmost to dissuade him from his intentions and to persuade me to send him away; his wife also sided with them and cursed her husband in a most distressing way. However, Ramayya remained firm and all the relatives finally departed. The wife stayed a few days, but took herself off with the child later. Ramayya stayed with me for about three months unmolested and showed great earnestness and made good progress in learning the Christian faith. But while I was in camp for a few days a message came from his village that his old mother had had an accident and was dying, and besought a sight of her son. Ramayya believing the message to be true went to see his mother, but found that the message had been a ruse to get him back home, and that his mother was well!

"Since then Ramayya has never returned to Bezwada. His relatives seem to have done him no physical harm, though they succeeded in dissuading him from being baptized for some four years; but in 1921 he made the decisive step and was baptized together with his wife and child. Later on fifty other caste people from the same village were also baptized."

In many villages the friendly relations between the masters and their Christian servants, have created an atmosphere in which even high caste men and women have found it possible to take the serious step of breaking caste and joining the Christian Church. The village of Raghavapuram, the home of Venkayya (whose conversion is described in chapter II) is a case in point. When Venkayya was baptized, the Brahmans of the village refused to allow even caste servants of the missionary to draw water from the only fresh-water well. A well was, therefore, dug in the village to supply the outcastes with water. Some time afterwards there was a great drought. The river and all the wells in the village went dry. There was one exception and that was the Christians' well! The Brahmans came to Venkayya for relief. "Lend us your well," they pleaded. "We will draw water for you as well as for ourselves." With a true

Christian spirit Venkayya and the other Christians decided to hand over the well to the caste people till the rain should again fall. While the drought lasted there was no lack of water in the Christians' well both for caste and outcaste people. A friendly relationship was thus opened up between the Christians and non-Christians, which for fifty years has never been broken. This kindly feeling is bearing fruit to-day.

In November 1928 the authors of this book went to Raghavapuram for a baptism. On Sunday morning there was a celebration of the Holy Communion in the village church. Among the communicants were the representatives of nine different castes, ranging from Brahmans to outcastes. In the congregation there was a young woman dressed in a bright-coloured silk *Sari*, with her husband and a number of his female relations. She belonged to the highest caste of Sudras in the village and was a Christian. Her husband was not yet a Christian, but she was teaching him herself and hoped soon to bring him to baptism. The female relations were Hindus, but had so far advanced towards Christianity that they had no objection to sitting with outcastes in a Christian church. Twenty years ago a scene like this would have been almost inconceivable. In the afternoon 175 people were baptized and of these 152 were caste people. A few days after we went on to a neighbouring village where 300 people were baptized, of whom 150 were caste people.

In another area, where during the last seven

years the Church membership has doubled, over 400 caste people were enrolled as catechumens in one year and 150 of them have already been baptized.

Recently in a group of four villages, where there has been a large Christian community drawn from the outcastes for many years, a remarkable movement has begun among the caste people as well. Already about 70 have been baptized from five different castes, including the highest of the Sudra castes in the Telugu country. Many of them are very well off, owning from 10 to 50 acres of land. Their keenness is very striking. They want a good school with eight classes established at once and are prepared to find a good part of the money. "We would give it all," they said, "if it were not for this persecution." The persecution started when they decided to become Christians and took the form of an attempt to deprive them of their land. The lawsuits in which they were involved cost them about £225, a very large sum even for well-to-do people in a village. They are very eager to learn more about Christianity themselves; some of them proposed that they should go to the headquarters of the deanery in which they live or to Dornakal itself for two or three months during the hot weather, when there is no field work to be done, in order to get instruction in the Christian faith. They will probably learn in three months what it ordinarily takes one or two years to teach the outcastes. They do not seem to have any difficulty about abandoning caste. A few of them came to Dornakal and were baptized. They eat with outcastes food prepared by outcastes without any hesitation. The one point about which they were uneasy was the Anglican marriage service. "It is so cold and much too short!" Their own marriage ceremonies last about a week and are full of significant symbolism. A twenty-minutes service with strange, meaningless ritual was a real stumbling-block. However, it was explained to them that this could easily be altered. A form of marriage service was hastily sketched out which would last at least two hours and which fairly satisfied them.

In this group of villages there are in addition to those already baptized, about 2000 more caste people, many of whom are already attending services, receiving instruction and anxious to join the Church.

MEDAK[1]

The recent conversion of about 3000 caste people in the Wesleyan mission district in the Hyderabad State is a striking illustration of the strength and wonderful possibilities of this new movement. It is the more remarkable because the work of the mission among the outcastes only started in earnest at their headquarters in the town of Medak about thirty years ago. In 1895 there were only about 2800 baptized Christians in that area, nearly all

[1] This section is taken entirely from information kindly supplied to us by the Rev. C. W. Posnett, the senior Wesleyan missionary in charge of the Medak area.

gathered from the outcastes. Now they number about 60,000.

The movement among the caste people began five years ago. It started in the extreme north of the district on the banks of the river Godavery, and was due mainly to the influence of an Indian evangelist and his wife backed by the simple faith and devotion of many of the poor outcaste Christians. An outbreak of plague drove the whole population of one of the villages out into the jungle to live in booths. The Hindu priests deserted their people. The Christian teacher and his wife went with the villagers and ministered with great courage and self-sacrifice to the sick and dying, Christians and non-Christians alike. That made a profound impression on the caste people of that and other villages.

Later on a small band of Wodders, who are a caste just above the outcastes, came to Mr Posnett begging for baptism and for a teacher, and for many months they paid for one amongst themselves. The teacher left them, but one of their own number still taught them to pray and sing. They habitually called themselves Christians and regularly subscribed to the Mission funds. After about three years Mr Posnett visited that part of the district. He was greatly struck with their forceful character, their earnestness, good habits and splendid record.

So he baptized about 600 of them during this visit. "I never," he wrote, "met any people who were better prepared and more thoroughly fit to be received into the Church. When we asked them to pray, one after another they got up and simply but earnestly put their petitions before God, and the way in which they told the story of the death and resurrection of Christ in some of these villages was a perfect delight to hear. One young man describing in his own words the story of the resurrection was so vivid and did it so well that the great crowd of caste Hindus who were there to watch listened spell-bound to the story. I never had a better opportunity of preaching to caste Hindus. These baptisms were not done in a corner, but all the caste village had gathered to see and to hear."

Mr Posnett gives the following account of the movement in other villages on the banks of the Godavery.

"I was there more than a week last month and I never saw such earnest seekers after God. We stayed in camp at a small town, called Ibrahimpatnam with about 4000 inhabitants. Every evening we had a congregation of 2000 caste people who had been under instruction for baptism for about eight months. They were splendidly prepared, they knew the story of Jesus, and they could sing our hymns one after another. They had broken away from caste and had accepted three of our outcaste evangelists and received them into their houses.

"During the day I went from house to house to visit them and talk about Jesus with them in their own homes. To my amazement when I came to the house of the chief farmer, who is a very high caste man, and looked up at the carved wooden doorway of the house I saw that right in the middle of the top of the door he had actually chiselled away the image of the Hindu guardian goddess of the home, called Vignasvarudu. To those of us who know the caste people of India and the powerful hold of idolatry, it seemed almost a miracle that these beginners should have cut away this image from their homes before their baptism. None of us knew anything about it and they had done it in every house entirely of their own accord. The Indian ministers who were with me were amazed to see such a thing and were all convinced that this was a sign of their sincerity that none could doubt.

"All day long whilst we were in camp there were groups of other people, both caste and out-caste, coming from all the surrounding villages. They had nothing whatever to gain, and they knew that they would have to face persecution, but they had already begun to learn about Jesus Christ and they simply would not leave me until I promised to try and send them an evangelist. I should think there must be twenty villages here on the banks of the Godavery where they are already learning from the visits of our outcaste teachers; but they say: 'We cannot read and we cannot remember if we are only taught once a week. We must have an evangelist and his wife to come and live in our midst.' There is no doubt at all that this is true. Hardly any of these people know how to read; it is absolutely necessary to have a teacher who can teach them, regularly hold services for them every evening, and teach the children to read the Bible. I am not willing to baptize 4000 people this year and then leave them to forget all about Jesus Christ. If we are to receive these people it is our duty to teach them thoroughly and to give them Pastors and Evangelists who will really build up a great Christian Church in their midst.

"Meanwhile the movement had spread to many other villages round Medak itself and all over the district. In 1926 a five-days' convention was held in the mission station at Medak for high-caste Hindus who were anxious to hear more about Jesus Christ. The missionaries did not expect more than 20 or 30, but altogether 150 assembled, among them three or four Patels (headmen) and one Brahman Karunam (village accountant). Special preparations had to be made for their food and accommodation; but it was a wonderful thing that so many caste Hindus came to spend four or five days in what was practically an outcaste settlement and that everything went off happily without the slightest unpleasantness.

"Day by day during the convention there were songs and stories from the life of Christ, and the visitors listened to the singing and preaching with profound interest. Many of the converts from different castes gave their testimony to the power of Christ in their own lives.

"At the conclusion of one of the addresses on the third day the speaker asked those who were going to be Christ's disciples to say so, and one after the other got up and said 'I will give up idols from to-day and will pray to Yesu Swami (the Lord Jesus) henceforth.'

"One dear old man said: 'I have given up my idols and I shall never cease to worship Yesu Swami though I have to starve, and though the crows eat my flesh I will not deny Him.' I may add that this man right through the meetings had been determined to be a Christian out and out and begged us to baptize him publicly on Sunday morning. The Friday morning meeting was really wonderful. It was so spontaneous that you could not but believe that God was in our midst. The confessions were so brief and so earnest and simple that it really took my breath away."

Some of them wanted to be baptized at once, but it was thought better that they should go back to their own villages and be publicly baptized there. The sequel came a few weeks afterwards when fourteen people from different castes were baptized by immersion in the river Godavery.

Six months later, Mr Posnett had the great joy of baptizing in the Godavery another band of converts from the caste people. They came in procession to the place of baptism led by the Christian outcaste drummers. When they arrived at the camp, "at once it was clear," writes Mr Posnett, "how keen and brave they were—all so happy and bright—some beautiful little children. There was one wonderful old lady, who was the leader of them all, with her sons, sons-in-law and relatives to the number of thirty-three altogether.

Amongst them were two of the men who came to the Summer School in Medak last May and who had never ceased to witness till to-day when they were to be formally baptized in the name of Jesus.

"The singing was splendid, the old lady and the little children all joining in and beating time with their hands—their faces beaming with joy. They knew the hymns, the Lord's Prayer and the Life of Christ, and when they were asked whether they were ready for baptism, there was a unanimous answer, even though Brahmans and others were all standing round listening. I asked them if they were prepared to be turned out of caste, to be troubled about marriage and to be persecuted in a thousand ways; but however I tried to put the difficulties before them they answered that they had already counted the cost and made their decision.

"The old lady who was the leader had made such a bold testimony that all the country round knew about her decision. She had been a sort of priestess to Shiva and had had the direction of all the great sacrifices, receiving by right a special basket of rice from every threshing floor. She also was the priestess of a special society, but she had been so disgusted with their secret impure rites that she had denounced them. Some of these rites were particularly revolting and the strange thing was that they broke caste in these secret drunken revels and let themselves go without any regard to decency.

"When her son-in-law came from Medak Summer School and her own daughter began to speak of becoming a Christian she thrashed her and would not have the evangelist coming to the house, but still she was unhappy and dissatisfied. At last she got the teacher's wife to come to her secretly and inquired about Christ and gradually learnt the Gospel story. Then she determined to throw up her post as chief priestess and to stop taking the holy begging basket, which she and her fore-mothers had used for getting their share of every harvest. She publicly burnt it and told every one who was there that she had determined to become a Christian. She said: '*Until then I had no peace and I lived asleep in the darkness; but now my life is full of light and I am awake. I have worn out my forehead in the dust before the idols which I had always been the first to worship, and they never did me any good, but Jesus has now come and brought peace to my heart.*' You could see it in her face. It was lit from within by the light of the Saviour's love.

"The headman of the village was there and he had not a word to say. Appadorai, my Indian colleague, publicly called upon him: 'O Patel (headman), are these people doing right?' and he said, 'Yes, they are. Yours is the Truth,' and a little later he asked us to come to his house and pray over his sick daughter who he said was possessed by a devil."

Another convention for high-caste Hindus who were seeking Jesus followed in May 1927. It was even more remarkable than the one held in 1926. The following is Mr Posnett's account of it:—

"Once more we have invited to Medak all high-caste Hindus who were seeking Jesus. Twenty years ago they would have considered themselves polluted by eating in our compound, but for three days they have been our happy, friendly guests, not a single grumble has been heard. Men who used to cover up their hands with a cloth to shake hands threw their arms around me. Women, who are always the last to give up idols and old customs, travelled 100 miles to come in the hot weather. They had a dreadful journey, but no one complained. Every hour of the day has been filled with the one subject, 'The Call of Jesus.'

"On Sunday morning we had a *Love Feast* of broken cocoanuts and sugar (the Hindu sacred symbols of love), which the Hindu leaders first brought up with their thankofferings so that we might bless the trays. Every man gave a thankoffering, and then they took the trays and distributed with their hands both to the caste people and to the outcastes. After the service I asked those who were really determined to confess Christ and to follow Him to come and talk it over with us quietly. Quite fifty people came straight away to my house and for two hours we talked together. They counted the cost and shirked nothing. Some of them spoke with the greatest determination and courage, others said they would first persuade all their family and call us to their villages. But some were very eager to be baptized at once in our Church. Its perfect, simple beauty has greatly appealed to them, in fact no one can calculate the immense influence that this beautiful Church has had upon all these people. Their behaviour and reverence were a perfect joy and they wanted to be baptized there. So we chose out eighteen about whom we felt quite certain and promised the rest to come to their villages when their families were ready.

"The first to be chosen was a Brahman village chief—a man of good position and great influence. He had already seen others in his village baptized, but I had never dreamt that the day might come when he too would kneel humbly at the feet of the crucified Saviour. Yet he had travelled 120 miles to be here, and this morning he came forward first of all to give his witness at the Baptism Service. The whole crowd of 220 visitors were there and they listened spell-bound as he confessed that he had gradually come to know that Jesus Christ was the only Saviour, and, whatever it might cost, he was prepared and determined to delay no longer. He then knelt down at the steps of the font and I baptized him with the name of John at his own wish, for he had read and loved the Gospel that appeals so much to Indians. After the baptism he came and asked if he might take 'Prashatham,' the feast of friendship, with me. He was a Brahman who had never in his life touched water from a Christian hand or drunk from a Christian's glass. He had been taught from boyhood that this was horrible pollution, yet when I poured out the water he begged me to drink first and then he quietly took the glass and drank it to the bottom, pouring the remaining drops upon his head—then kneeling down he asked me to bless him. Anyone who knows India will not wonder at my amazement; to drink after anyone from the same cup is anathema; but for a Brahman to drink from an outcaste's glass is simply amazing beyond words. This man had broken away from Hinduism at one stroke and had acknowledged Jesus as his only Master.

"The congregation that had listened and watched this Brahman's testimony and baptism were greatly moved. Many said to me afterwards they had never seen such a baptism service in their lives. When he had returned to his place, the remaining seventeen high-caste Hindus, all of them men of solid position and respected in their villages, came up in small groups and our Indian ministers baptized them in turn.

"Twelve months ago this work for which we have waited and prayed for 100 years in South India began. Our first confessors are standing firm to-day in the midst of bitter persecution, but this has not hindered the coming of the Kingdom. The numbers are slowly creeping up and we are looking forward to a great ingathering amongst these privileged leaders of Hinduism. God has given us the outcastes in tens of thousands and now He has crowned all by this wonderful drawing of the high-caste Hindus to Himself. No one can tell where it will stop, but we all know that if we are faithful it will become an immense strength to the Church of God in Hyderabad.

"During the last three years about 3000 of these caste Hindus have been baptized and 3000 more are under instruction for baptism, and this in the face of bitter and relentless persecution."

CHAPTER VI

THE CONVERSION OF THE ABORIGINES

THE power of the Gospel of Christ among the aboriginal tribes of India and Burma has been almost as remarkable as its power among the outcastes. According to the Government Census they number about 11,000,000. They live apart in separate areas, mainly in the hills and forests of Central India, Assam and Burma. Their conversion to Christianity, therefore, has not as direct an influence on the Hindu and Mahommedan peoples as that of the outcastes who are scattered throughout almost all the towns and villages of India. But the transformation of their lives is a striking witness to the power of the living Christ, and the simplicity and independence of their characters will, under the influence of the Holy Spirit, enable them to make a very valuable contribution to the faith and life of an Indian Church.

About 600,000 of the Aborigines in different parts of the Indian Empire have already been converted to Christianity and the number of converts is rapidly growing. The largest Christian communities are in Chota Nagpur, 260,000 ; the Santal Pargannahs, West of Bengal, 35,000; among the Khasis and Lushais in the hills of Assam,

120,000; and among the Karens and other aboriginal tribes in Burma, 170,000. But a considerable number of the Bhils in the western part of Central India and of the aboriginal tribes in the hills of the south-west coast have also become Christians during the last half-century.

Strong testimony is given not only by the missionaries but also by Government officials and others to the changed lives of the people through the influence of the Gospel.

A Bengali writer, not a Christian, speaking of the work of Christian missionaries in Chota Nagpur says: "The most careless observer can tell the house of a Christian convert of some years standing from that of his non-Christian fellow-tribesman by the greater cleanliness of the Christian's house and the general neatness and orderliness of everything about it." The contrast, he says, between Munda and Oraon Christian men and women, boys and girls on the one hand, and, on the other hand non-Christian Mundas and Oraons at their feasts and elsewhere is a visible sign of "the brilliant achievements of the Christian missions in their noble work of civilizing and educating the aborigines of Chota Nagpur."[1]

An experienced missionary who has worked among the Karens of Burma for many years states that Christianity has "transformed them beyond all recognition." Before the coming of the Gospel they were quarrelsome and violent, always fighting among themselves, split up into hostile clans,

[1] *The Mundas*, p. 168, by Babu Sarat Chundra Roy.

ignorant and intemperate. Under the influence of Christian teaching they have become peaceable and united, sober and educated, inspired with a real missionary spirit which leads them not only to convert their own people to faith in Christ but also to set about the conversion of the Burmese Buddhists.

The testimony of Government officials and missionaries alike to the changed lives of the tribes in the Santal Pargannahs is equally striking.

The Lushais

The Government Census of 1921 gives the following account of the spread of Christianity among the hill tribes of Assam.

"Perhaps one of the most marked features of the decade (1911-21) is the extraordinary progress made by Christianity in Assam. Mr Lloyd writes: 'In the Khasi and Jaintia Hills a sixth and in the Lushai Hills over one-fourth of the population are now Christians. In the Khasi Hills, where the movement is oldest, the increase has been only 31.6 per cent., possibly owing to curtailment of staff and work in war time by the Welsh Calvinistic Methodists, the principal body working there. The spread of Christianity in the Lushai Hills is phenomenal. There has been a sort of revivalist wave over the whole Lushai population. . . . In a district of 7000 square miles, sparsely peopled by less than 100,000 people, there are now 27,000 Christians where ten years ago there were only 2000. At present it is quite the fashion to be a Christian and even the Chiefs are joining the movement. At first I was inclined to cast doubt on the accuracy of the figures and suggested that zealous Christian enumerators might have made entries according to their own wishes rather than the facts. The superintendent, however, thinks the case is rather the reverse. Mr Scott has tested many entries himself and he quotes an instance of the rigorous standard adopted by the new converts; the five-year-old son of Christian parents being entered as an Animist because the young scoundrel was so greedy that he failed to say grace before meals!' "

In 1921 Mr Lorrain, one of the senior missionaries of the Baptist Missionary Society in the Lushai Hills, wrote:—

"Forty years ago the whole of this forest-covered, mountainous district was still under the pall of age-long darkness. Satan held supreme sway. The people, believing that his emissaries lurked everywhere in order to do them harm, spent all their religious energies in seeking to appease these malignant demons. They were in a very real sense captives and slaves of the Powers of Darkness. For all but a few favoured folk there was not even hope of a happier life in the Great Beyond. 'Dead Man's Village' was the soul's destination; but before reaching there the ordeal of passing the half-way house of the dreaded 'Papawla' and being pelted with pellets from his unerring bow-like catapult, must be undergone, and the wounds inflicted by these stinging missiles must through all the future ages fester and burn without hope of remedy. Even the favoured few, who, because of their prowess in head-hunting raids or in the chase, or because of the merit acquired through giving a number of public feasts, were entitled to pass Papawla's house without molestation, and to cross the Pial River beyond 'Dead Man's Village' and to enjoy the delights of the Lushai Paradise—even these were often assailed with doubts and fears as to whether after all their passport to the Happy Land would hold good, and for them as for the rest of the people there was no light to cheer the darkness of the tomb.

"But even then God was at work in opening up the way for His salvation to be made known. Repeated raids into British Territory had brought about the taking over of the Lushai Hills by the Government, whose officers proved to be veritable pathfinders for God's Messengers.

"Soon after this one of the chiefs had a dream, he heard a voice saying to him, 'A great Light will come from the West and shine upon Lushai: follow the Light, for the people who bring it will be the ruling race.'

"In the morning he gathered together his family and many friends and told them of his dream. 'This Light,' he said, 'may not shine in my lifetime, but when it comes, follow it.'

"In 1900 Mr Rowlands, a missionary of the Welsh Calvinistic Mission came to visit this village and to tell the people of the Love of God revealed in Jesus Christ. To his surprise he found attentive listeners and when he asked if there were any who would wish to give in their names as inquirers he was amazed to find that several came forward as volunteers. He warned them that to follow Christ would inevitably mean suffering and persecution and might lead to eviction from their village by the chief and possibly death; but they would not be denied, and when in due course trouble did come, it merely served to strengthen their faith. 'Did not the white man say it would be so?' they declared; 'therefore his teaching must be true; this is the light of the dream.'

"Two Baptist missionaries, Mr Savidge and Mr Lorrain, began work in North Lushai in 1893 and in four years learned the language, reduced it to writing, and translated two Gospels and the Book of Acts. They wrote hymns, a catechism, a simple primer, a grammar, and produced a dictionary of seven thousand words.

"They left the Northern territory to the Welsh mission later on and started work in South Lushai, which is a wild, forest-covered, mountainous region with an area of 2700 square miles and a population of about 28,000 people, living in about 166 villages, all situated on the tops of the mountains. In 1903 there were about 125 converts, to-day the Christian community numbers about 10,600, scattered over the country in 110 different villages; so that more than one-third of the people are now Christians and there are Church congregations in more than three-fourths of the villages."

In 1920 Mr Lorrain wrote: "As I look back on the last ten years I see how wonderfully God has been working to bring about the blessings which so many enjoy to-day. The Great Famine of 1912 caused by an invasion of rats, the pneumonia epidemic and remarkable revival of heathenism in 1914, and the War which drew so many of our untravelled hillmen to France and Mesopotamia were all overruled by Him for good. But by far the greatest factor in the work has been the presence of God's Spirit in the midst of His Church, manifest more especially in 1913 and 1919-20 in mighty power. It is a fact which should be recorded that since the first out-pouring of the Holy Spirit upon the Lushai church in 1907, every six years has witnessed a similar but ever-increasing pentecostal experience, empowering believers for joyful and fruitful service, and greatly affecting the heathen as well. Each gracious visitation has raised the church on to a higher plane of Christian experience than the one preceding it and has resulted in a large ingathering of souls.

"These last ten years have witnessed marked progress in church organization and activity. In 1914 a modified Presbyterian form of Church government was adopted, elders were elected, and the first Lushai superintending pastor was ordained, followed in 1915 by two others. In the same year a Summer School was inaugurated on the Mission Station for the annual instruction of the honorary pastors of village churches. In 1916 the New Testament in the language of the people was completed. In 1918 a class was started for the training of candidates for the ministry (evangelists and superintending travelling pastors), and in the same year a new era was ushered in by the arrival of Nurse Dicks and Miss Chapman from England for medical and educational work amongst the women and children. In 1920 the first Lushai woman evangelist was appointed by the church, followed this year by a second. Both these workers are supported by a special fund raised by their Lushai sisters for the purpose."

Among the aborigines, as among the outcastes, the history of the Church is never one of uninterrupted progress. Floods, famines and epidemics are visitations that often bring periods of depression, and from time to time strange "tidal waves of sin" sweep over the Church.

"But whenever we are tempted to get downhearted," writes one of the missionaries in a recent report, "we have only to take a retrospective view of what God has done for the Lushais and adjoining tribes since January 1894, and straightway we find our hearts beating with renewed courage and hope.

"It was then that my friend Savidge and I, after three years of patient effort, succeeded in gaining an entrance to the North Lushai Hills. From the breezy height upon which we first pitched our little tent there stretched away on all sides to the horizon, range upon range of forest-covered mountains, with villages perched here and there upon the most inaccessible peaks. We two young missionaries of the Gospel were there to claim the whole beautiful land for God and His Christ—a land which for ages had been in the grip of demon-worship, and where tidings of the world's Saviour had never penetrated. Our hopes were high, but how far short they were of God's wonderful plans for these tribes! The years of rough pioneering and wrestling with the unwritten language soon slipped away, followed by the coming of the Welsh Mission to North Lushai, and our own eventual transfer to South Lushai under the auspices of the Baptist Missionary Society. Then, when the Gospel message had gained a firm foothold in the Lushai Hills, both North and South, the gift of a copy of the Lushai Gospel of St John, by one of the Welsh Missionaries, to a visitor from a neighbouring tribe, led to a call for Christian workers in those regions beyond. The missionary spirit of some of the North Lushai converts was roused and volunteers were soon forthcoming, and thus began a movement which has developed into the North East India General Mission, which is now occupying strategic centres and outposts among several different tribes beyond the Lushai border. The work is unique, for it is almost entirely run and staffed (though only very partially financed) by Lushai and Kuki Christians, with but a single European in Calcutta as superintendent of its far-flung field—the very missionary whose gift of a printed Lushai Gospel was instrumental in starting it seventeen years ago. In looking through a long list of the workers in that mission I count 81 superintending pastors and evangelists, 76 schoolmasters, 5 dispensary compounders, and 4 printers; and I rejoice to find among them quite a number of our South Lushai converts who have, through this organization, been able to find a real opening for their missionary zeal. Three of them are holding posts of great responsibility and privilege, and others are doing good work as schoolmasters and missionary-evangelists. One of these latter—a splendid young fellow named Lianthawnga—has recently laid down his life for the people among whom he laboured. The climate was bad and he suffered continually, but he would not think of relinquishing his work. At last, when he came back to us for a holiday, his health was so shattered that he passed away, leaving a young wife and little son to mourn his loss. So rapid has been the transformation of the Lushais from head-hunting savages to Christian missionaries, that, when Lianthawnga and his colleague first went to the Bawm tribe, the people would not receive them. They believed that they had come to 'spy out the land' preparatory to organizing a bloodthirsty Lushai raid such as the older folk still remembered. Their fears were not really set at rest until two men got their wives and families to come and join them in their work. The accompanying table will show at a glance the wonderful work God has done amongst the Lushais and neighbouring tribes, where thirty-three years ago the Saviour's name had never been heard."

	Christian Community.	Full Church Members.	Sunday School Scholars.
North Lushai (Welsh Mission)	35,577	15,660	21,222
South Lushai (B.M.S.) . .	9,935	3,484	4,811
Outside Lushai (N.E.I.G.M.)	9,959	3,754	5,338
Totals .	55,471	22,898	31,371

The Bhils

The following account of a movement among the Bhils, an aboriginal tribe in Central and West India, illustrates the strange ways in which God works and the still stranger instruments that He uses.

"In 1886 Dr Shepherd began those cold-weather tours in the Bhil country which he continued without break to the end of his service in 1920. The camp moved through the rugged, roadless hills under the triple aegis of a Bhil safe-conduct, a survey map and a pioneer axe. In these days there was no presumption of safety for the life and property of the wayfarer. The famine of 1868 had revived the marauding habits of the Bhils, while it had also so reduced the population that there was little or no co-operation amongst the isolated remnants of the people. So the 'padri sahib' was passed from hand to hand, from glen to glen, by chiefs somewhat anxious over meeting neighbour and enemy at the boundary. The young men of the glen slept round his tent at night, and the aged chief watched alert, hunched grimly in the shadow beyond the camp-fire light. Dr Shepherd's camp was never raided, partly because of that unceasing watch and ward, partly because the healing influence which his tours were to exert began to have effect at once. Bitter enemies met at the borders to demit and assume responsibility for the padri. There was Huarji of Sera; Amri, the woman chief of Paduna; Kawa of Lori Madri; Lakhma of Pai, whose grandson was married in 1927 under Christian rite in the Bhil country; and Dewa Damar of Saldari, the father of Poona. These, and many another, wild hill folk, fearful of one another and of all mankind, gave their confidence to Dr Shepherd.

"On his advice, they sent their boys into Udaipur for education. Amongst these boys was Poona, second son of Dewa Damar. He stayed in the Bhil Home till 1891, when, a grown man of eighteen or so, he returned to his country. He was not baptized. Others came and went up till 1904. Some were baptized. One of them is now pastor of the Udaipur congregation. Another, Manji, has been a wanderer since 1904, never coming near the Church, although sometimes in and out of Udaipur hawking firewood. A wizened figure of a man, unmarried, he spent his spare cash on drink and his sober times, when money was not, on poring over his Bible. One evening some ten years ago, I met him where the Udaipur road ends and the Bhil track begins. Wearily putting his eight-foot bundle of wood off his head end-up on the ground, this haggard wisp of humanity told me that the prophecies of Daniel were shortly to be fulfilled and that the beginning would be in the Bhil hills.

"All unknown at the time, 1891 was a great date for Udaipur. For Poona, unbaptized, unpersuaded, left the Bhil Home. For thirty-one years he was to remain so. The Bible he took with him disappeared; his memories of Christianity became vague, but his education he used and retained. He saw the dreadful famine of 1900 and the lesser one of 1906. He saw the Bhil risings of 1917 and 1921. What was his part in either of these no one will ever know. But, son of the shrewdest Bhil of night or day, his dreams were of better days for his people. In 1922 he began teaching the doctrines of one God and one True Teacher ('Sat Guru'). His recollections of Christianity seem to have been limited to that, for he neither taught, nor seems to have remembered the name of Christ. He quickly gathered disciples. Their greeting to one another was, and is, 'Jai! Sat Guru!' (Hail, the True Teacher). Every disciple on joining the brotherhood paid twenty pence to Poona. It was a 'gift in God's name.' In Hinduism the food offered to the god is called 'parshad.' This twenty pence was 'parshad,' therefore; but Poona called it 'the Lord's Supper (Prabhu Bhoj).' This went on till 1925.

"In 1925 Manji heard of this Brotherhood of the True teacher. He walked twelve miles over the hills with his Bible, met Poona and the disciples, read Genesis i and ii to them and asked them whether any other book had such knowledge of the very beginning of life. They acknowledged the claim. Then Manji said, 'This same book tells you who the Sat Guru is. His name is Jesu Messiah.' He further told them that they must get the 'guru chhap' (seal) on their forehead, and that the padri in Udaipur was the one to do that. So Poona and his disciples came to Udaipur in 1925 for the seal on their foreheads. They were not in any way, except desire, ready for baptism, and such temporary arrangement as was possible was made for instruction. Memories became clearer in Poona's mind. He began studying and teaching the Bible, for he was a lettered man. They ploughed through the books of Moses, trying to live the life of the Book. They gave up eating hare and pig when they came to that law. They had all become teetotalers at the beginning and are still. Manji did not delay long to direct their attention to Daniel.

"Early in 1926 the first thirteen were baptized, Poona and twelve disciples, having more than satisfied the Udaipur Session as to their readiness. Before the end of February 1926, 73 adults and 37 children in all had been baptized. Maqbul Masih, who had had twelve years experience of the Bhil country in another district was sent out as Mission agent. For him the Bhils of Pai built a house. His parish is 26 miles long with a very rough range of hills, 9 miles wide, intersecting it. It takes him five days' tour merely to visit his flock. Only to give the necessary religious instruction to these people is more than one man can do; and there are young lads who wish to learn to read and write as well. Maqbul has 16 such scholars in ones and twos throughout the glens. But those who have learned a little become teachers of those who know less. At Pipalwas, I found a youth of fifteen, handicapped by a painful stutter, who had taught his chum to read with a complete Hindi Bible as their only textbook. Some of the double letters they had never been able to guess, and my visit was a chance to clear up such mysteries. So Maqbul, with Poona's zeal plus the willingness of the Bhils to be taught, has achieved a further addition to the number of Christians. In 1927, 38 adults and 60 children (some of them 16, 17, 18 years of age) have been baptized. The large number of children is due to the baptism of the families of parents admitted in 1926. Altogether there are now 204—42 men, 54 women, 57 sons, 51 daughters. Four men have been admitted to full membership of the Church. Only four, but what understanding they have of the Cross!

"And here a strange thing emerges. Poona, himself, has not become a full member and is, I think, avoiding it. When Maqbul went out and when the converts began to understand their new faith more fully, the giving of twenty pence 'par-shad' ceased. The first 73, however, had paid and Poona maintains that he and they have 'partaken of the Lord's Supper.' Poona is probably a little jealous over the trend of the movement. If it is not that, it is, perhaps, that the son of Dewa Damar is a Bhil of the Bhils, absolutely intolerant of any dictation, hostile at once to any suggestion of authority. Manji, alas, has lost all his reputation, partly through his drinking habits, partly because the Bhil Christians would have none of his interpretation of Daniel. He is not counted as one of them; otherwise he might again plead the authority of the Book.

"A most interesting thing happened in connection with Manji's reading of Daniel. Somehow, in certain wanderings of his, far afield from Rajputana, he had picked up the views regarding the prophecies which belong to the ultra-apocalyptic school. He pressed these views on the Bhil Christians. They gave him a hearing and unanimously condemned his views as 'not in accord with the teaching of the rest of the Bible.' I heard this long after. Manji has now (1929) completely abandoned his drinking habits."

What the movement will grow to it is impossible to forecast, but when we consider the difficulties that this small body of Christians had to encounter and their determination in overcoming them, coupled with their simple faith and reverence for the Scriptures, we feel that a Bhil church will have an important contribution to make to Indian Christianity.

CHAPTER VII

THE EVANGELIZATION OF INDIA

In his *Mission and Expansion of Christianity* Harnack has traced from early Christian writings the factors that operated for the spread of the Christian religion during the first three centuries of its history. At the very outset of his investigation he makes this significant remark. "It was by preaching to the poor, the burdened, the outcaste, by the preaching and practice of love, that Christianity turned the stony, sterile world into a fruitful field for the Church."

History repeats itself and this same experience is again being reproduced in India. A brief review of Harnack's points will show how far conditions in India to-day are similar to those in the Roman Empire.

1. The first factor in the successful issue of the Christian propaganda, says Harnack, was the varied character of the Mission-preaching. It was not the preaching or understanding of Christian dogma in any complete sense that was effective. "In countless instances it was but one ray of light that wrought the change." "One person," he goes on to say, "would be brought over by means of the Old Testament, another by the exorcising of demons,

a third by the purity of Christian life; others again by the monotheism of Christianity, above all by the prospect of complete expiation or by the prospect which it held out of immortality or by the social standing which it conferred. As long as Christianity did not yet propagate itself naturally, one believer may well have produced another."

Very similar are the causes that lead to the expansion of Christianity in rural India. Here, too, the causes are varied. Different aspects of the Gospel appeal to different people. The fact that it has been preached to and accepted by the poor outcastes of Hindu society compels many to give their serious consideration to those elements in this religion that produce such a striking change in its followers. The monotheistic ideal in contrast to the village gods of the Hindu polytheism; the high ethical demands made upon the followers of Christ, the promise of salvation or deliverance, not from re-births but from sin, the teaching of immortality and resurrection; the doctrine of the Cross, the knowledge that the supernatural Ruler of all things is a Father of Love—these are the elements that compel attention from the Hindu observer. All these have in one form or another appealed to the outsider. What, however, has made that appeal effective is, not the statement of abstract doctrine, philosophically demonstrated, but the doctrine clothed with flesh and blood in the lives of the poor and illiterate villagers.[1]

[1] See *The Influence of Christ in the Ancient World*, pp. 96-98 By T. R. Glover.

The immediate causes that lead to the conversion of villagers are various. One caste convert confessed that what first appealed to him was the joy and happiness of the Christian people as evidenced by their songs, praises and thanksgivings. Another high-caste man became a Christian attracted by the message of the resurrection and the practice of Christians burying their dead. Some caste people are drawn to Christianity by the fact that Christian worship consists, not only of worship without the aid of images, but also of instruction in godliness and morality. But the divine message makes its most irresistible appeal when it is incarnated in experience. Incarnation is God's method of saving the world.

2. Another factor in the spread of Christianity in the early centuries was the proclamation of the Gospel as a gospel of redemption. Celsus declared as lucidly as one could desire the cardinal difference between Christianity and the ancient religions. Christianity, he said, offered the Kingdom of God to anyone who was a sinner, a thief, a burglar, a poisoner, or a sacrilegious man. "Why!" he said, "if you wanted an assembly of robbers these are just the sort of people you would summon!"[1]

That is exactly what is sometimes cast in our teeth in India; but that was the glory of Christianity in the Roman Empire, and it is its glory in India to-day. Repeatedly converts say in effect what Clement is said to have written: "He bestowed on us the light, he spoke to us as a father to his

[1] *Harnack*, p. 104.

sons, he saved us in our lost estate. Blind were we in understanding, worshipping stones and wood and gold and silver and brass, nor was our whole life aught but death."[1] The foregoing chapters afford illustrations that the Gospel of Christ is still the gospel of redemption. These transformations are the living forces of the Gospel of the Saviour: these miracles of grace are the divinely appointed signs to India.

3. A third cause of the expansion of the religion of Christ in the first three centuries is said by Harnack to be the character of Christianity as "the religion of the spirit and of power; of moral earnestness and holiness." In the first sixty years of the history of the Church, the outward and visible manifestations of the gifts of the Spirit were most conspicuous, and they existed all through the second century though in a diminished volume. During the third century, however, these ceased almost entirely; though this cessation hardly inflicted any injury upon the mission of Christianity. The evidence of power then as in the days of St Paul was "that God had not called many wise after the flesh, nor many noble, but poor and weak men whom he had transformed into morally robust and intelligent natures." "The entire labour of the Christian mission," continues Harnack, "might be described as a moral enterprise, as the awakening and strengthening of the moral sense. The conflict undertaken by Christianity was one against the sins

[1] 2 Clement. 1.

of the flesh, such as fornication, adultery, and unnatural vices, and it exhibited to the Roman world a hitherto unknown example of personal purity. This is abundantly proved by the writings of the Apologists and other early Christian writers. *Aristides* asserts most forcibly the high moral life of the Christians. *Diognetus* speaks of the love of the Christians to one another in such glowing terms that it puts us to shame. *Athenagoras* says: 'Among us are uneducated folk, artisans and old women, who are utterly unable to describe the value of our doctrines in words, but who attest them by their deeds.' "

When Celsus urged that " Christians must admit that they can only persuade people destitute of sense, position, or intelligence, only slaves, women and children to accept their faith," Tatian replies: " Not so! Our maidens philosophize and at their distaffs speak of things divine." Justin says: " Among us you can hear and learn these things from people who do not even know the forms of letters, who are uneducated and barbarous in speech, but wise and believing in mind, though some of them are even maimed and blind. From this you may understand that these things are due to no human wisdom but are uttered by the power of God."

These factors that operated so strongly in the early centuries of the Christian era are operating with equal power for the rapid spread of Christianity in India to-day.

One of the most important lessons, therefore,

that we have learnt from the movement among the outcastes is that by far the most powerful evangelistic agency in India is the witness of the Indian Church itself. In the preaching of the foreign missionary the Kingdom of God comes in word. In the life of the Christian Church it comes in power. There is no testimony so convincing as the power of transformed lives. It has been so from the beginning.

A very striking illustration of the evangelistic forces latent in the Christian community in India comes from the Punjab. A splendid work has been carried on among the strong, virile and independent Moslem tribes of the North-West Frontier for many years by both Anglican and Presbyterian missionaries. The chain of mission hospitals on the frontier have done a magnificent work. But for some time the missionaries were seriously concerned by the lack of success in the matter of converts. The building of an indigenous Church had been practically at a standstill for fifty years. The missionaries, therefore, met together recently and prayed to know what was the reason for this and to find out God's will. Gradually it became clear that the problem of the evangelization of the Moslems is the preparation of a Church both to win the harvest and to take care of it. The reason for their lack of success had been their neglect of the Indian Church. So they called the elders together and put before them this duty. The work of preaching was then handed over to the Indian Church and a yearly campaign was planned lasting a week, in which every Christian was to take part.

It was at once discovered that an aggressive, awakened Church was by far the most effective evangelistic agency. "In one city where regular bazar preaching had been efficiently carried on by the missionary without the result of even one inquirer, when it was taken over by a band of Indians of the local church, volunteers for the work, inquiries were made after every service. The Campaign week, with the handing over of definite evangelistic work to the Indian Church, proved successful in bringing in many inquirers all over the Rawal Pindi district, where previously for years there had been no baptisms. Since then there has not been a single year when some at least of those who came forward did not go on to confession by baptism."

The second discovery was the value of the out-caste Christians for evangelistic work, even among the Moslems. No one had thought of employing them for so hard a task. "They are a very mixed lot, many of them still ignorant and dirty. . . . The cleaning out of the filthy open drains of an Eastern city does not tend to elevate the mind. . . . Somehow no one had faith to believe that they could be of use to God at all. . . . But gradually in answer to prayer, nothing less than this was borne in on men's minds. It was to be these Christians from the Mass Movements who were themselves to be the agents used by God to work among the Moslem people; they were to be the aggressive Church. . . .

It was found that there are thirty-five or more of these groups of humble Christians north of the Jhelum, that is, in the North Punjab and on the North-West Frontier. Through the foolishness of God, which is wiser than men, they are settled in many places where there is no other Christian witness, and in some cases (such as in the fort of Landi Kotal at the summit of the Khyber Pass, and in Manzai, an armed camp actually in Waziristan), where no other Indian Christians would be able to live. They are sweepers, and there must be sweepers for the troops. They are in the most improbable places to find Christians, and actually paid by Government to work there. Government is obliged to forbid proselytizing in Indian regiments, but they must have sweepers; and, if these be Christians, here is at once the only influence that can touch the Indian Army.

"In certain schools and colleges where the only religious teaching is Islamic, Christian sweepers are employed. . . . Whether in border cities such as Peshawar and Kohat, or in the peaceful country districts of the Punjab, sweepers are a necessity. The great advantage is that they are scattered everywhere, and are not confined, like most missionary effort has been, to the school, the college, and the hospital in the larger cities.

"Then, too, they are not sensitive. The sweeper is used to rebuffs and bad treatment at any time. He carries on. He is one of the things which are despised, but it appears he is one of those whom God has chosen to use. They are far from perfect, these sweeper Christians; fighting, immorality, and other sins exist among them, yet even a man who is ignorant and not too upright may be used to sell gospels, and we find that these men have, on the whole, sold far more than the educated. It is worthy of note that almost every convert has originally been drawn through buying a gospel portion.

"At one place several young Indians of wealth and good birth came as secret inquirers. Through a servant of very humble birth, who could not himself read, they had heard, and bought, and then read for themselves. In a British regiment the sweeper boot-boys sold about one hundred gospels and testaments to the British soldiers; and a number have been already sold to the Indian troops in the same way by the sweepers."[1]

The experience of the Missionaries in the Telugu country has been exactly the same. They taught the Brahmans and higher castes in school and college and preached to the caste people in town and village for many years with very little result. Then God called the outcastes. An Indian church came into existence and bore a powerful witness to Christ. And now through that witness many thousands of the caste people are being brought to faith in Christ.

[1] *C.M.S. Review*, June 1927. Article on the Afghan Frontier by Mrs Underhill.

CHAPTER VIII

CONCLUSIONS

THE main conclusion that we draw from the facts stated in the preceding chapters is that the one thing needful, the one thing of absolutely vital and essential importance in India at the present time is the thorough education, training, equipping and inspiring of this rapidly growing Church to enable it to go forward with faith and power to achieve the tremendous task of winning India for Christ. Nothing else can compare with this in importance. It is the one thing upon which the educated Christians in India and the missionary Societies of the west need to concentrate their thoughts and plans, their energies and resources. If this task is done thoroughly and well, all else will follow. If it is not done well, or worse still not done at all, all else that is attempted by the missionary Societies or by educated Indian Christians will be of little value for the furtherance of the Kingdom of God.

It is a task of great magnitude and peculiar difficulty. Year by year many thousands of the outcastes and aborigines are being swept into the Church. And in South India the new movement among the caste people promises a still more rapid increase in numbers and a whole sheaf of new problems in education and pastoral care.

In view of these facts it is high time for the missionary Societies in the west and the Church in India itself to overhaul their machinery and see how far it is adequate not only to present needs but also to the larger work of the future.

First, there is the machinery for village education. It obviously needs considerable extension even now. According to the census of 1921 only about 25 per cent. of the whole Christian population, Indian and European, in town and village, was then literate. In the villages alone the percentage is very much smaller. It is difficult to find out what number of Christian children are at present at school, as many of the missionary Societies give no statistics on this important point. But in the Dornakal diocese there are 17,000 out of a Christian population of about 160,000, rather more than one-tenth. In European countries it is reckoned that about one-sixth of the population are of school-going age. There is, therefore, room for considerable extension in the Dornakal diocese. And education is far less advanced in many of the village areas where the Christian Church is established than it is in Dornakal

But a far more serious question than the extension of education is the provision of a kind of education suitable to the villages. Parents will not send their children to school beyond the first two or three classes because they feel, and in most cases rightly feel, that the education given is of no use to village folk.

CONCLUSIONS

The Report of the Indian Statutory Commission on Education in British India, presented to Parliament in October 1929, says with regard to Mass Education: "Even when we make all possible allowances and discount the figures liberally, the hard facts of wastage and stagnation are shocking."[1]

"On the assumption which we have made that on the average no child who has not completed a primary course of at least four years will become permanently literate, we find that, taking British India as a whole, the present system produced in 1925-26 only eighteen potential literates out of every hundred who joined Class I in 1922-23." In other words 82 per cent. of the education given in the village primary schools was largely wasted.

The "hard facts" of missionary education in the villages may not be as bad as this: but even in them the wastage may well be termed shocking. For example, in the Anglican diocese of Dornakal there are 1500 village schools with about 17,000 Christian pupils enrolled. Of this number 87 per cent. are in the first two standards and 97 per cent. are in the first three standards. In a report of the Wesleyan Mission in the Hyderabad State it is stated that out of 6147 children in their schools, 5650, that is 91 per cent. of the total, are in the infant and first classes. These statistics show that a very small percentage indeed of the pupils reach the fourth class and are likely to become "permanently literate."

This state of affairs is, with few exceptions,

[1] Report, p. 48.

universal in the village primary schools of the Christian Churches throughout India. And the reason for it is that the education given in village schools is out of touch with the conditions of village life.

Experiments are now being made in most rural missions to rectify the main evils of the present system. Vocational schools and industrial schools are being started and efforts are being made to bring the schools into close touch with village life and make the education given in them to bear directly upon the welfare and uplift of the rural community. What is needed in order to establish a better system on these lines is:—

i. A body of educational experts, men and women, from Great Britain, Europe and America, and, we would add, from India itself.

ii. A more highly trained and better paid body of teachers, both men and women, who know the conditions of village life.

iii. A new curriculum, which is not simply the first rung of a ladder leading up to high schools in the towns, but which is designed to play an effective part in rural reconstruction and directly promote the prosperity and well-being of the villagers.

This improved system of primary education will undoubtedly cost more money than the existing one; but it is better to spend more money on an education that will be really useful to the Christian Church and will also make a valuable contribution to the regeneration of village life in India, than to go on spending a much smaller sum on a system that involves a waste of over 80 per cent. of the money and labour expended.

Then secondly, there is the pastoral work. In the building up of the life of the Church the ministry of the word and sacraments is of primary importance. The Church cannot be built up apart from the Christian life of its individual members. The Christian life of the individual cannot ripen and fructify apart from the Church. If the Church in rural India is to be an effective witness for the Lord, attention must be paid to the spiritual condition of the individual and the Church. At bottom, the problems of the rural church are spiritual problems. Given a passionate devotion to the Lord and a love that constrains men and women to bear witness for Him, self-support, self-government and self-extension become easy problems to solve. How can this spirit be fostered?

i. By the Ministry of the Word. "The entrance of Thy Word giveth Light"; and the foundation of all spiritual life is the knowledge of God's will and purposes as revealed in the Scriptures, in our Lord Jesus Christ and in the Church. The important rule in all rural work is Teach, TEACH, TEACH. Daily services, carefully planned lectionary, the use of song, verse and plays as means of instruction, distribution of literature—all these are indispensable means of increasing in the people the knowledge of divine things.

ii. By the Ministry of the Sacraments. We believe that the sacraments are gifts of the Lord to His Church. The sacrament of Holy Baptism is the sacrament of entrance into the sacred Fellowship and the sacrament of the Lord's Supper that of intimate communion with the Lord and with one another. The Apostolic Church "broke bread" daily during the early days of the Church and later it was their custom to come together to break bread each Lord's Day. How can we expect our Christians to grow strong in their devotion to the Lord, if we deprive them of the sacrament of holy communion? It is, however, a fact that a large proportion of baptized Christians do not have a chance of coming to this oftener than once in two or three months. The breaking of bread in each church every Lord's Day is impossible as long as we confine the celebration to a highly-trained pastor who often has ten to twenty separate and distant village congregations to minister to. And yet the Indian people are sacramentarian by temperament and religious training. We know of nothing that inspires devotion, touches the emotions and strengthens the will of the village folk so powerfully as the reverent and intelligent observance of the sacrament of the Lord's Supper.

At present the provision made in almost all rural areas for this regular, systematic ministry of the Word and Sacraments is woefully inadequate. Even in the Dornakal diocese, where there are about eighty Indian clergy, at least sixty more are required to minister to the existing congregations; and new converts are coming in at the rate of 8000 a year.

But here, again, there is the difficulty of increased cost. The people cannot at present pay the salaries of both teachers and pastors, and it is not desirable that the pastoral work of the Indian Church should become increasingly dependent on foreign money.

Has not the time come when vigorous experiments ought to be made to make village work independent of outside support, standing on its own resources? The following measures are suggested:—

i. Serious attempts should be made from the initial stages to make the converts build their own places of worship, and their own village schools. All Oriental nations have a passion for temple-building. Indian Christians are not free from it. This passion should be fostered and the people ought to be encouraged to build a place of worship—plain or ornamental, cheap or expensive—something which they can call their own.

ii. An unpaid, honorary ministry for the Church should be systematically developed. Men with independent means should be encouraged to give of their service freely to the Church. The ambition to serve the Lord "without charge" must be inculcated in boys who learn a trade, so that when they go back to their villages they may undertake as honorary workers the responsibility for the local congregations. Village elders, too, ought to be encouraged to learn to read and to teach, so that they may lead the worship and instruction in the village of which they are the natural leaders.

The ordination of such village elders and honorary workers, commissioning them to administer the sacraments, has been vigorously advocated by the Rev. Roland Allen in his well-known books on mission policy.[1] Doubts have been expressed as to the practicability of these proposals for rural India where illiteracy dominates. But Mr Allen's main contention need not be set aside simply because of the abnormal conditions at the initial stages of mass movements. The encouragement of the honorary ministry ought to be the aim of all rural missions.

We have only touched briefly on the most outstanding needs of the village work at the present time and in the immediate future. But what has been said above will be sufficient to show both the magnitude and difficulty of the problems that confront us in the great task of building up the Church in India. Does it not also show the urgent need for both foreign missionaries and Indian Christian leaders alike to concentrate their resources and energies on this main issue on which depends the future of Christianity in India? This concentration does not necessarily mean that methods of work which have been employed in the past should be entirely abandoned; but it does mean that they should all be brought to bear directly upon and made more

[1] *Missionary Methods—St Paul's or Ours?*; *The Spontaneous Expansion of the Church*. Both published by the World Dominion Press, 1 Tudor Street, E.C. 4.

effective for the one main purpose—the building up of the Church of Christ.

For example, the present system of higher education was started by Dr Duff nearly a hundred years ago with a view to the conversion of Hindus and Moslems in the cities and larger towns. At that time it was assumed that Christianity would first be accepted by the *intelligentsia* and would filter down from them to the masses and spread from the towns to the villages. This assumption has been proved to be fallacious. But to-day High Schools and Colleges are needed partly to produce leaders for the Christian Church, and partly as strong centres of Christian life and light to influence the non-Christian *intelligentsia*. And it is clear that for both purposes our institutions need a far more intensive Christian atmosphere. The delegation of the Church Missionary Society that visited India in 1921-22 said in their Report: "The essential thing in mission education is the creation of a Christian atmosphere in its institutions." And they added: "We have not yet, nor have we the power to produce the far-spreading Christian atmosphere that should pervade all our institutions." The Society cannot under existing conditions secure a sufficiency either of Christian teachers and tutors or of Christian pupils to produce such an atmosphere. The first thing needed then is to reorganize the system so as to make this possible. Till that is done we cannot expect the institutions to be effective instruments either for the education of Christians or for the conversion of non-Christians to faith in Christ.

So, again, with regard to medical work. The mission hospitals were originally established mainly in the towns at a time when there was very little provision of medical aid for the mass of the people either in town or country. But to-day they are far more urgently needed in the village districts, especially in areas in which there are large numbers of Christians. They have an important part to play there in the social, moral and spiritual progress of the village Church. At the present time Government hospitals and doctors are provided for almost all the large towns, and it is not uncommon to find a mission hospital in a town where there is a well-equipped Government Hospital, while thousands of Christians and non-Christians in adjacent villages are left without any medical aid of any kind.

It is the same with the evangelistic work. Seventy years ago this was regarded as the special province of the foreign missionaries and was carried on over many areas with little or no relation to the Christian community. The illustration given above from the experience of the Missionaries on the North-West Frontier reveals the weakness of this system.[1] Professor Harnack and Dr Glover, as we have pointed out above, emphasize the truth that in the Roman Empire it was not the mere preaching of the word, but the witness of changed lives that enabled the gospel of Christ to triumph over the ancient world.[2] That was true, says Dr Glover,

[1] See Chapter XII.

[2] See Chapter XIII; and *The Influence of Christ in the Ancient World*, p. 96. By T. R. Glover.

even of the preaching of the Apostles. "The witness of the resurrection was not the word of Paul (as we see at Athens) nor of the eleven; it was the new power in life and death that the world saw in changed lives." What is needed in our evangelistic work in India to-day is to bring this new power to bear strongly and effectively upon all classes of Indian Society. To do so will not only make evangelistic work more effective, but, what is even more important, will greatly develop the missionary zeal and foster the spiritual power of the Church itself.

It is natural to shrink from such a large reconstruction of our methods of work; but it is long overdue. We have already in the past lost many golden opportunities. There is no reason why what has been achieved in the Telugu country or among the Lushais should not have been done with equal power and similar results in many other parts of India. In a recent report of the Santal mission it was stated that there were 8000 Christians connected with the Anglican Church and might have been 80,000. But it is useless now to lament over what might have been. Many doors are still wide open. It is still a great day of opportunity. But if opportunity is persistently neglected, the day comes at last when the door is shut.

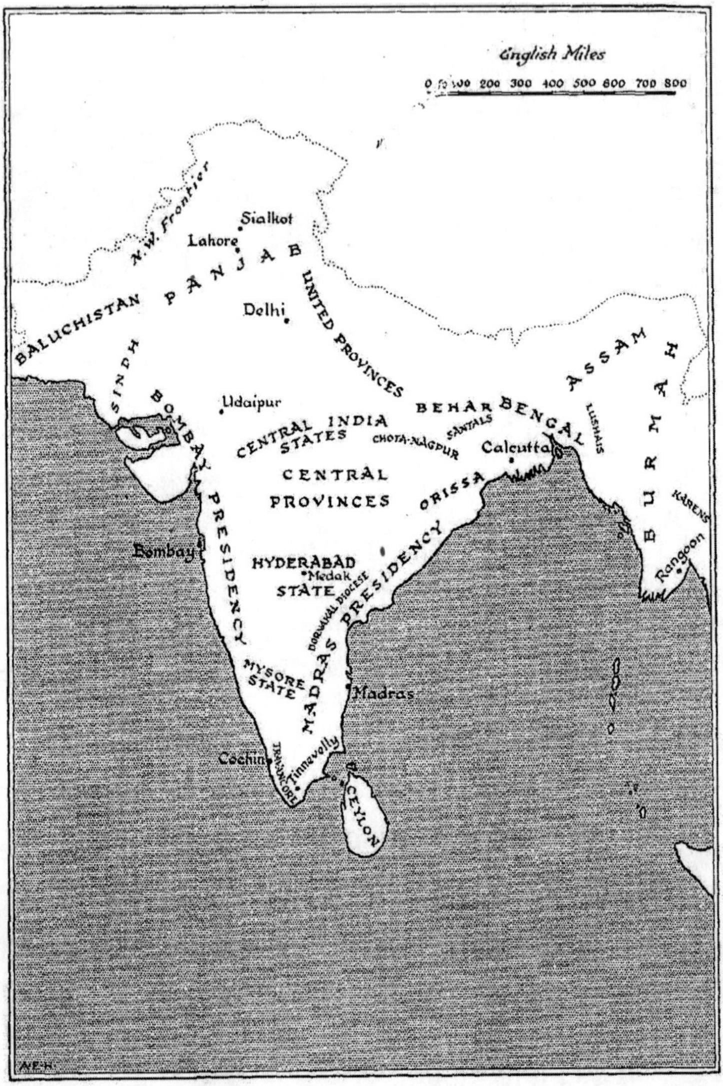
English Miles
0 50 100 200 300 400 500 600 700 800
N.W. Frontier
Sialkot
Lahore
PANJAB
BALUCHISTAN
Delhi
UNITED PROVINCES
SINDH
BOMBAY
Udaipur
CENTRAL INDIA STATES
BEHAR
BENGAL
ASSAM
BURMAH
SANTALS
CHOTA-NAGPUR
LUSHAIS
Calcutta
CENTRAL PROVINCES
ORISSA
KARENS
PRESIDENCY
Bombay
HYDERABAD
Medak
STATE
DORNAKAL DIOCESE
MADRAS PRESIDENCY
Rangoon
MYSORE STATE
Madras
Cochin
TRAVANCORE
Tinnevelly
CEYLON
A.E.H.